Views from the Bike Shed

Writing for Bloggers

Mark Charlton

DOWN DEEP BOOKS

Published by Down Deep Books
an imprint of Cinnamon Press,
Office 49019, PO Box 15113, Birmingham, B2 2NJ
www.cinnamonpress.com

The right of Mark Charlton to be identified as author of this work has been asserted by him in accordance with the Copyright, Designs and Patent Act, 1988. © 2023, Mark Charlton
Print Edition ISBN 978-1-78864-804-2

British Library Cataloguing in Publication Data. A CIP record for this book can be obtained from the British Library.

Designed and typeset in Adobe Caslon by Cinnamon Press.
Cover design by Adam Craig © Adam Criag
Cinnamon Press is represented by Inpress.

Acknowledgements for quotes

The quote from Jim Perrin's *West* (Atlantic Books 2010) is by kind permission of the author.
The quote from John Knapp-Fisher's *Pembrokeshire* (Senecio 1995) is by kind permission of Gillian Pare.

Contents

Notes on Selection

In the days when I was a serious painter my old friend and tutor, John Skinner, used to contend there were three reasons for holding an exhibition. The first was to see your own work afresh; the second was to sell some paintings and attract new patrons. But the third, and most important, was something less tangible: it was, he said, to say, '*Come and see what I've found!*'

And so the transition from paint to words.

My intention in compiling this collection has been to showcase those pieces that on re-reading seemed of most merit. But, mindful of John's advice, I wanted also to share my journey from stumbling beginnings to more mature blogger, and in so doing, to illustrate how blogging can accommodate a variety of styles, allowing for experimentation and the occasional misstep.

As a consequence the selection is not so much a 'best of' as it is a 'typical assortment'. Furthermore, I was conscious that several of my blogs have been published elsewhere including in my own collection *Counting Steps, a journey through landscape and fatherhood*. Of these, I've included only those that are most important to the overall story.

The order of presentation is roughly, but far from precisely, chronological. In some cases I have made adjustment to the original to allow for the absence of photographs or other contextual references; very occasionally I've added a further explanatory note. All of the pieces have had some light editing and are better for it, though I have not returned to the blog to revise them online.

On which note, I hope readers will also visit viewsfromthebikeshed.com where there are many more blogs waiting to be discovered. If you do, then please leave a comment to connect. And should you be inspired to start a blog of your own, send a link to say '*come and see what I've found too!*'

Happy blogging

www.viewsfromthebikeshed.com

FOREWORD

There is always a moment in Mark Charlton's writing. I mean, there are lots of moments. He gives them to you with a generosity that appears to know no bounds. Quite often seemingly small moments, offered almost in passing. The scent of his son's hair or a snatched conversation in the car. A philosophical thought as he wheels down an Alpine pass on the back of his racing bike, or a detail from an obscure Welsh mining village that no one else would notice.

Whatever shape they take, these moments are when his writing takes flight, rather like the butterflies he has long obsessed over. When the reader is carried beyond Mark's world and begins more fully to inhabit their own, because, thanks to his careful prose, suddenly some detail of their lives comes into sharper relief, makes just a little more sense, is imbued with some deeper meaning.

That's how it has always been for me, at any rate. Mark first handed me a copy of *Counting Steps*—his previous volume for Cinnamon Press—almost as an aside. We were working together on a corporate rebrand and enjoyed sharing stories of our extra-curricular writing over scalding coffee in the staff canteen. I already knew him to be a master craftsman thanks to his careful and deliberate copywriting on our project. I had rarely encountered someone who wrote with such precision.

What I hadn't expected was the extent to which his craft would result in narrative essays and life writing of exquisite beauty. In blogs that I devour in my downtime, simply to snatch a few minutes in Mark's company, to spend a moment in his moments, knowing that doing so will deepen the richness of my own.

None of this happens by chance. In that respect, Mark is again different from many of the other writers I know. Not for him the callback that announces itself to the author with the same element of surprise as it does to the audience. I certainly have my share of these, marvelling at the good fortune I've experienced in being able to retrace my steps, completely by chance.

For Mark, happenstance is always planned. Or so it seems to me. His writing is finely wrought, much edited, and always bang on the sweet spot for whichever emotion or reaction he wishes to evoke. Nostalgia, sorrow, joy, the bone-aching love of a parent for their child. All these and more are found in his prose.

Which is why Mark is a natural blogger, why it is a format in which he truly has found his voice. In just handfuls of words, published in the jostling-for-attention marketplace that is the internet, *Views from the Bike Shed* has found an audience—and an impressive and dedicated one, at that.

This is because Mark knows exactly what he's doing. The intellect behind countless financial reports and corporate press releases finds the allure of the 500-worder irresistible. It is his catnip, offering the challenge of conveying information and meaning with elegance, economy and elan.

So he rises to that challenge, and rises further still to deliver something that is beyond blogging, yet very much the medium at its finest. Beyond because it resists solipsism or mere reportage to gesture in new directions, to inspire new thoughts. And the finest because it is the apogee of disciplined writing, with clear (though so subtle) structure, tidy syntax and exhibiting the utmost self-control. No word is wasted. No phrase offered just in case it lands.

I have learned such a lot from reading Mark's blogs and talking to him about them. So have my students at the University of the West of England, where he is a much-valued friend of our Creative Writing department. If you want to see the value of blogging to your practice as a writer, I say, read *Views*. If you want to find out how to blog well, read *Views*. If you want to see the best in the business, read *Views*.

Such is my joy, therefore, to see this volume in print. It is a carefully produced book that will entertain and inform—one that has already shaped my own work as writer and teacher. It is full of moments, packed to the gunwales with them, in fact. They are Mark's moments, drawn from the dizzying eclecticism of his life and interests.

Thanks to his craft, his sheer writerly discipline, we are able to do more than simply locate our own lives by reference to them, however.

By following his example and learning from his process, we can write our own moments. And then, if we are lucky, perhaps our words will take flight, like Clouded Yellows in the cliffs above Mark's beloved Porthgain, attracting admirers all of their own.

Tim Gibson

For my grandfather, Septimus Charlton,
whose love was unconditional, as was mine

Views from the Bike Shed

INTRODUCTION

I suppose you have to start somewhere.

Those were the opening words of *Counting Steps,* my collection of essays published by Cinnamon Press in 2012. The sentence referred to the beginning of a journey, in particular, a backpacking trip along the crest of the Preseli Hills with my eldest son. That walk—and the events it encompassed—would change our relationship for ever, securing bonds that are tied only through shared experience. It would transform my writing too, teaching me that the inner journey is what matters most, and that the outer paths we follow—no matter how spectacular or prestigious they may seem—are but a means to that end.

And yet, as with all of the seminal events in our lives, it could so easily have been different. Writing these words in my study I'm wondering how things might be if only it had rained that morning; if Jane hadn't wanted us to go; if I'd been too busy with work? Would I have walked a different route with Daniel, would we have returned ten years later to repeat the experience; would *Counting Steps* have been published? So much of what appears to be forged by our will is actually a collision of choice and circumstance that's beyond our control, if not entirely our shaping.

It was much the same with *Views from the Bike Shed.*

'You should start a blog,' my tutor had said; a throwaway suggestion on a residential writing course I could easily have ignored. And yet, from that single intervention—and the tentative exploration which followed—I've travelled a road of chance and discovery that's shaped the person I've become. For blogging, like all writing, creates its own dynamics: the coming together of thoughts and words, of writer and reader, of ear and voice—sometimes resonant; often out of tune.

This book is about my words and their particular music; to some extent it's also a record of my praxis as a writer. But to believe it could ever have been planned would be a grave misconception. Blogging as a writer—and writing as a blogger—is happenstance on acid.

Consenting to providence, however, is not the same as abandoning care or quality. Indeed, I've found the best of blogging's serendipity comes from those posts which are most deeply felt and thereby make the closest connection with others. My use of the word providence is more than a mere synonym for happenstance, for one of its meanings is 'a timely preparation for future eventualities'. That those outcomes are unknown at the time in no way diminishes the need to make ready.

It's often said that the process of writing has a magic to it—that words have a way of finding their own direction. Painters will know something of this alchemy, recognising how marks find their form, and how, as creators, we're never sure of our destination until we arrive. But what I have come to learn through *Views from the Bike Shed* is how that magic can be multiplied; how blogging's particular labyrinth leads us in directions we could never have imagined—and how, along the way, it's possible to acquire a wealth of practice and resilience I would not swap for a more conventional route.

At the time I received it, my tutor's suggestion was as much disappointment as surprise. Was she taking me seriously I wondered; what sort of writer did she think I was; and what exactly was a blog anyway? The prospect of sharing my work online, of being open to comments, of the technical wizardry (I imagined) would be required... All this was at odds with my image of the author as introverted thinker, researching and journaling, waiting to be discovered...

These worries are typical concerns of those starting out. I know this from the queries I receive and the interest shown by students at the University of The West of England where I've been privileged to occasionally lecture these last few years. But imagine if I'd pondered them too long; if instead of Googling 'how to start a blog', I'd returned to an essay or gone for a walk, finding a different direction...

Almost certainly I wouldn't be the writer I am now.

As it turned out, *Views from the Bike Shed* was soon more than a suggestion, finding a purpose, form and direction of its own. My original intention, from which my tutor's suggestion arose, had been to write about cycling, recording the progress of my middle son who at the time was one the UK's leading junior racers. It's as good a theme as any

18

for a blog, but beyond my first post (replicated in this book) I don't recall typing more than a few words on that subject.

Instead, *Views from the Bike Shed* evolved in the manner of one of those walks we take without purpose, wandering here and there, taking joy in what we encounter... If what we find interests us, we return, perhaps from a new direction, certainly at a different time. And if we go there often enough, before we know it we might say to a friend or partner, 'Come and see what I've found.'

And this, perhaps more than anything, is what *Views from the Bike Shed* has become: a collection of findings, that I hope have quality too, not so much for me, but for blogging as a process and form that I've come to love and which deserves more attention.

I guess the purpose of this introduction is to get us started. Sometimes, as writers or painters, we do best to simply take our pen for walk on the page. In many ways there is no other plan. Structure your approach if you like, consider your themes, set boundaries and take inspiration from others. But first you must begin, for only then will the journey unfold.

November Reflections

My first ever post: the one that I had intended would start a blog on cycling. I publish it here not so much for its merit as to show how we might begin, and perhaps, if I'm honest, with a fondness born of nostalgia.

Where did November go?

I seem to have missed it this year. November marks the end of the cycling year. As the nights close in the racing schedule gradually dies away and evening rides become ever more snatched. By the time the clocks go back the season is all but finished. Only a few diehards turn out to the peculiar torture that is the round of autumn hill climb championships, a simple activity that consists of riding up the steepest imaginable hills in the shortest possible time, usually in the driving rain.

Thinking back, I once won the Tandem Club's championship for doing just this up Horseshoe Pass, assisted by a partner with a crude indifference to pain. And for those who really don't know when to stop, I suppose there is always the cyclo-cross season, which requires much the same disregard except, this time, to sanity. For cyclo-cross is all about riding rough shod bikes through muddy fields until you are head to toe in muck and the whole contraption—usually body and bike together—breaks down.

But for most cyclists, November involves sitting down with the latest edition of *Cycling Plus*, scanning the rehashed articles on winter lighting and reflective clothing—*Be seen; Be safe*—and the hearty encouragements to keep you riding through the depths of winter—*Your Ten Step Guide to Winter Training*. November isn't so much about riding; it's about cleaning the club trophies and electing the Committee; it's about old pedants proposing absurd resolutions at the AGM which nobody cares about but lead to a row anyway. Most of all November is a time for winding down and reflecting on the year just gone.

In my case it's been a paradoxical one. I've cycled less than at any time in the last decade and yet I'm probably more involved than ever before. After years of avoidance, I joined on the dreaded Committee, organised a packed youth programme and spent the best part of the summer chasing round the country taking my son to races. To keep track of it all I had a colour coded year-planner on the wall of my study; there wasn't a free weekend all summer.

For Michael it was meant to have been a season of transition. The previous year he'd won all but a handful of his races. This time around he'd moved up a category and was racing against older and more experienced riders. 'We'll take it easy,' I'd said, and see how he gets on. My wife knew better. 'So you'll be off every weekend then.'

As it turned out we were both wrong. At his first race was in March, it was sheeting hailstones and we huddled in a shelter as he rode at some godforsaken airfield to finish ahead of only a handful of competitors. He found the new category difficult at first but by the early summer was racing well, getting reasonable results in the national events and riding particularly fast on the velodrome. Then in May he broke his jaw, falling off a BMX bike on an evening which was meant to be fun but became, in a single slip, the most frightening of my life. He recovered quickly but, in a way, it was a wake-up. I realised I was becoming one of those parents who, living vicariously through their children, lose all sense of perspective.

We backed off after that, skipping most of the major events. By the last weekend of the season we choose to ride locally rather than trek to London for the last of the national series. Looking at my diary I realised yesterday that we had made the ninety mile round trip to the velodrome over a hundred times.

It's ridiculous of course—and it can't go on.

And yet I know, here on a wet December morning, that to watch him riding with effortless grace, is one of my greatest pleasures.

Don't like, don't do, don't get

'Have you noticed,' I was ranting in the car the other day, 'That people don't dislike things anymore; they don't 'do' them instead.'

'They're not the same thing at all,' my eldest son Daniel corrected me. 'There are lots of things I don't like, but there are only a few I don't 'do'.

'And there are some things I don't 'get',' piped in Michael, my second boy.

This seemed like an interesting idea, so I probed a bit.

Disliking things was straightforward. The boys took the opportunity to reaffirm that they *really* don't like sprouts; neither do they like their French teacher, and for that matter they don't much like girls—at the moment anyway. For my part, they reminded me, I don't like Harry Potter, visiting castles on rainy days, or being disturbed at the computer. We each had our own list that took some time go through.

It turns out that 'not to do' was something quite different. 'Not to do' means not so much to dislike, as active avoidance. More than that, in some cases it means you won't even contemplate the idea. 'I don't do pizza,' said Michael, 'there's nothing that would make me eat it.' And after years of cajoling, subtle persuasion, bribery even, I can agree: he doesn't 'do' pizza! Our lists were shorter this time; Christmas shopping was pretty high on mine.

But not to 'get', was different again. Not to 'get' means that no matter how hard you try, you simply can't comprehend the attraction at all. 'So it's not like when you don't 'get' the answer at maths?' I asked. 'Not quite, they told me, it's more that you don't know where to begin; you don't understand how anybody could possibly like it. 'Give me an example?' I asked. Opera, they replied. Good choice, boys.

I liked their distinctions and I liked it too that our lists got shorter as we went through each one.

We all have our dislikes, they are commonplace, they express our preferences (or at least one side of them) and to some extent they help define our personalities. If we liked everything, or if we all liked the same things, the world would be a less interesting place. And sometimes it's fun to list them; think of the *Room 101* TV show—there are so many things I'd put in there.

As for not 'doing' things, I think it's a useful concept. All but the most bigoted and limited can see the value in new experiences, and hopefully we give things a fair try before passing judgement. Those who turn their nose up at anything fresh, or back off at the first sign of unfamiliarity, limit their choices and ultimately their enjoyment in life. But to plough on regardless is equally daft. So there are certainly things I don't 'do' and I'm happier for it. Thankfully, there are not many, but having a few non negotiables seems no bad thing—especially when it comes to dancing.

I'd like to think there is very little in which I can't see any attraction at all. Musical theatre comes close; laddish banter defeats me; my wife, Jane, says I don't get empathy (I can't understand what she's on about). If I tried hard, I could list some others; obscure poetry perhaps, synchronised swimming. I'm not saying these are bad, it's just that try as I might, I simply don't 'get' the appeal.

The good thing is that this is the smallest of my lists. I want to make choices, and I want my boys to make theirs, based on an appreciation of all that life has to offer. No doubt we'll dislike a fair amount of what we try; we might even choose not to 'do' a few; but hopefully, there is very little that we simply don't 'get' at all.

I have always loved bikes

I have always loved bikes.

My mother bought my first from the bin-men; I'd spotted it hanging from the back of their cart as they passed our house. She paid them ten shillings and made me share it with my brother. It was purple and red with a step-through frame and a white sprung saddle. I learned to ride with stabilisers, removing one, then the other a few weeks later. When I first rode without them, I peddled straight into the back of a parked car, knocking myself out.

That bike gave me my first taste of freedom. I'd cycle down our tree lined road, turning right into Etal Avenue, then left to the cul-de-sac by the station, where I'd watch the children on the other side of the line, laughing as they sledged down the railway sidings on wooden boards.

Later I was given a green Hercules that had been standing for years. I spent weeks taking it apart, scraping the rust with brillo-pads, polishing the chrome. It had a three speed Sturmey Archer hub, but only two gears ever worked. Not that it mattered; to my eyes it had a cross bar, thin wheels and, most important of all, drop handlebars. It was a racer!

I soon learned that my Hercules was no racer at all, and that Sturmey Archer gears were the stuff of derision amongst the cognoscenti at school. Ten speed derailleurs were the right stuff; Raleigh Choppers were acceptable too—they were best for giving 'backies' and were popular with the kids from the railway estate.

You'd find it hard to buy a junior racing bike nowadays, though the Chopper is making a comeback, re-launched as a retro alternative to the mountain bike. My boys don't see the appeal.' 'It's like a girls bike,' they say. 'One wheel's smaller than the other. I think it's marketed at Dads— like those, who years ago, longed to ride on the other side of the tracks.

Happy Returns

I like returning to familiar places, be it to holiday destinations, restaurants or even the route I walk the dog. Given the choice of somewhere new or an old favourite, most times I opt for the latter. Jane likes to tell the story of how I once cut short an all expenses trip to Kenya to spend a week in the Peak District; friends react with incredulity, the presumption being that I'm missing out on opportunities and the delight of new experiences.

Judged by their terms this is undoubtedly true, but looked at another way they miss the point; for returning to familiar places is not necessarily about sticking to what's comfortable. In fact, it is often by returning that we see things anew, gaining fresh perspectives on what we presumed to know already. Most of all, returning to familiar places allows for a depth of response, especially to landscape and people, which can only come from deep association.

Yesterday I walked the cliffs above Porthgain; it is an old industrial village with a quaint mix of industrial archaeology, gentle harbour and a steamy pub that makes it a thinking tourist's hot spot. Like Dylan Thomas' fictional Llareggub, it has *a picturesque sense of the past, lacking in towns that have kept more abreast of the times*—though I sometimes wonder if anyone really believes the sentimental artists impressions on the heritage notice boards.

I quickly climbed the steps by the Pilot House to reach the disused quarries above the western cliffs, the horizon curving to the far end of Wales. It was cold, the fields pale and sheep-trodden, only gorse flowers brightening the greyness of stone, sea and sky. With my head bowed to the wind I was looking at little more than the path and its littering of sheep droppings. I smiled as I remembered how my dog used to eat them and how when I shooed her she'd dash into the culvert chewing away.

There's no particular reason to walk the culvert in preference to the path, yet a few summers ago it was there I saw my first Grayling butterfly, and returning since I've discovered that on good years Clouded Yellows concentrate on the leeward side. Yesterday, as I neared its end, I watched a Chough gliding on the ridge lift, above a cave that I once kayaked into on a surge of roiling surf.

I was remembering all this when unexpectedly Daniel and Michael strolled towards me: 'We thought you'd be here,' they said, 'so we came to meet you.' As we walked together, peering over the cliffs at a cold winter's sea, for a while at least, a familiar place was as new and full of wonder as anywhere could be.

This is the eleventh consecutive year I've been in Pembrokeshire at New Year. I wouldn't want to be anywhere else.

Interlude:
Blogging for writers

Before I (and you) get to the end of this book, I wanted to say a little about blogging for writers. For, *Views from the Bike Shed* has been a journey, and what is their purpose if we don't share what we've found?

And yet, in starting out, I'm more nervous than usual: keen to avoid the curse of the rambling essay; conscious that the topic could fill a book of its own—and perhaps most of all, anxious not to put myself on a pedestal or suggest the route I've taken is the correct or only one to follow.

Because of this, I've an urge to begin by saying what I'm not concerned with—to declare how I know or care little about coding or technology, how monetising blogging leaves me cold; whether beginners should use WordPress or Medium…

For those who can't get past these concerns, there's a plethora of information available elsewhere and little point me repeating it here. But if you're a writer—by which I mean someone committed to words—I'd suggest you to go there later, for what I have to say, comes before all of that.

In titling these interlude pieces 'Blogging for Writers' my emphasis is on the last word of that phrase. What interests me—and what I hope to explain—is how blogging can improve our craft; how its particular practice makes us better and more professional writers, and how its serendipitous possibilities lead to avenues and opportunities that are as joyful as they are unexpected.

But more than that, I want to issue a clarion call to put aside preconceived notions—prejudices even—so that we see blogging as a marvellous opportunity to reach readers, to launch a career, to make connections… to write for and be read by people you never imagined.

Yesterday morning, I was distracted by an email from a blogger in Indonesia. He'd read a piece that I'd posted the night before and was writing to thank me, including, as it happens, an order for my first book! It's not an untypical occurrence, though after fourteen years of blogging it still delights me that *Views from the Bike Shed* can have that speed of reach and response.

Later in the day I checked my blog's statistics on the Google dashboard—the first time I've done so in months. There's no count of the hours I've put in, no mention of any money earned (not that there would be); no deep dive into search engine optimisation...

Rather, what it shows, is that from my first tentative beginnings I've written hundreds of posts, received thousands of comments and attracted millions of viewers to my little piece of the Internet. That's vastly more than any book I've published, any article I've written, or diary I've kept. It buoyed me up to reflect on that, and made me think...

I've got something to say after all.

For Dylan

Five years. Has it really been that long?

It feels like yesterday and forever. So much life in such a short time. *Time Passes. Tick-tock, Tick-tock...*

So wrote Dylan Thomas, after whom you're named. I wished you his genius if not his weakness. You have his charisma already, and his bombastic ways—you sing like a Welshman too! But I forgive you your faults, as I always will.

Strangely, I can't remember your birth, perhaps because it was so early in the morning. What I do recall is bringing you home. And your brothers sitting on the bed; looking not touching, just as they were told—then gently, one at a time, holding your hand. They wanted you to wake, but you slept through it all, oblivious.

Oblivious too of the years of yearning, the three miscarriages, the nuchal scans, the waiting for results, the tests and more tests—and the waiting—always more waiting—until the final phone call. And when it came, the nurse asked if I was sitting down.

'All clear,' she said.

You see that's the thing about probability—it doesn't work in the real world. There is only one you and you were always perfect. Just like there's no probability or quantum for love: you either do or you don't; all or nothing, no half-measures. And every day you remind me of that simple, inexpressible, fact.

Happy birthday Dylan; it's the least and the most I can say.

Faience bowl

Somewhere, among the stacked assemblage of boxes in my new garage, is a small faience bowl, marked (allowing for incorrect spelling) with my Christian name, and given to me as a gift when I was two years old. My Great Aunt, on a tour of Europe and trip home from Australia, brought one for me and another for my elder brother.

I don't remember her visit, but I know I must have been a toddler because my younger brother hadn't yet arrived. This explained why, for all my childhood, only two bowls were displayed in the drawing room cabinet. And why also, when peering through the glass, I felt such great fortune that I was born in the nick of time to be given this valuable and mysterious treasure...

Such are the delusions of youth.

Quite why I still have the bowl is part mystery too. Most probably I asked my mother for it during one of her clear outs or house moves, but in truth, I can't remember. Whatever, it has been with me for thirty years and a half-dozen moves of my own. As far as I'm aware, it's the object that I've owned longer than any other.

The odd thing in my keeping it, is that I otherwise dislike French faience. The designs remind me of the worst on offer in craft fairs, and the figurative illustrations have a Protestant dourness, despite their gaudy colours. Even to describe the bowl as faience is probably incorrect. My Aunt had certainly travelled through Brittany, and perhaps visited the famous Quimper potteries, but the bowl is not stamped with their mark—souvenir stall trinket is more its likely provenance.

Perhaps that is why I make an exception for this particular example—it could sit as comfortably among my collection of kitsch as it did in my parent's china cabinet. Though paradoxically, I am still reluctant to use it, for fear of chipping an edge.

And it seems to me that our lives are a little like that. We surround ourselves with friends and objects that aren't rationally chosen or related to; but rather, they're a mash-up of chance and situation and memory (usually flawed)—and sometimes just a plain persistence of presence.

The objects we chose to treasure, perhaps because they don't change while we do, acquire a value which transcends objectivity—they root and remind us of where we are from and, in a curious way, help us adapt to the new. They become as much a part of ourselves and our sense of belonging as are the towns and houses we chose to call home.

Which perhaps explains, why the top of my list of New Year jobs, is a note to unpack those boxes in the garage.

Downfall

Thirty years ago, I walked the Pennine Way. In truth I only walked some of it, for I cheated on the harder bits and skipped most of the dull parts completely. It didn't matter at the time but it rankles now, so I've decided to walk it again, this time in sections. I don't care about the order I do it in; I just want to complete the path—to fill in the gaps, so to speak.

Perhaps also, I want to show my boys that I'm still capable, that there's more to Dad than the figure of fun you gradually become as they get taller and you get fatter. *Look—Dad's trying to climb the cliff!* I want them to remember me as a strong and physically capable man. That's a male thing perhaps, a middle aged one too I suspect—but a powerful feeling just the same.

It's curious how one day you swell with pride as they unexpectedly keep pace while you're running or cycling—and then before you know it, they've overtaken you without so much as a rearward glance. Soon you're relegated to holding their bags and cheering from the side lines. *Go for it boys—don't look back!*

The other week I was saying to Jane that I've been lucky enough—and I guess strong enough—to do some marvellous things. I've climbed mountains that most would never set foot on; kayaked rivers that even fewer would have the courage or skill to master. Indeed, when I think about it, I've run and cycled and swam and walked and painted and written and camped and travelled... So isn't it my boys' turn now? Shouldn't I be content to wallow in the vicarious pleasure of parenthood?

I was pondering this as we started over Kinder, Daniel skipping up Jacob's Ladder, my entreaties lost in the wind as I watched him bouldering on the rocks that litter the summit. When I eventually reached him, I was sweating from the effort and he was about to lope off across the newly laid slabs that cut a path across the moor.

I tried to tell him how it wasn't this simple when I was last here. 'You used to sink to your knees in the peat. It was all bog and mire and a dangerous place..' *Yeah, yeah… Watch out,* he called, *you keep tripping up on the gaps.*

At the Downfall on Kinder Edge, Daniel wants a drink. I take the bottle from our rucksack and he drops it in the stream. Jumping in to retrieve it, he soaks his boots and loses his glove in the collection pool. He looks forlorn and asks me to fish it out. Later, as we walk over the miles of slabs on Featherbed Moss, I notice that he keeps falling behind—more through boredom than fatigue.

And yet I press ahead. I want to reach the road, to cover the ground quickly; as if to set something right.

Stanage

I'm back again, scrabbling to find my kit, sheltering under the tailgate as I change into Ron Hills and pull on a thermal vest. My map flaps in the wind—it's the wrong one anyway so I shove it back in the rucksack. I'd given Jane directions to get here; *take the road by Ladybower reservoir, go up the hill and there should be a pull in by a sandy track heading up to the moors.* It hadn't changed since I last came here; nor had the wind, bitterly cold as it always seemed. I pull on a hat, stuff my cagoule in the bum bag and set off.

It's twenty years since I ran on Stanage Edge and yet it is all so familiar: the smell of the grit, the friction of the stones, the squelch of the rich chocolate peat when I miss my footing. As I run up the first hill, the sun begins to break through the mist; by the time I'm at the summit, the sky is a pale blue. The edge stretches ahead of me as I take off my hat and pause a moment to get my bearings; a grouse takes flight from the heather, its wattles flapping red as it crash-lands a few seconds later.

Stanage is the longest of the Peak District's gritstone edges, a five mile escarpment running from Bamford to the moors above Hathersage. It's famous for its rock climbs, but despite being a climber for many years I never much liked it as a crag. To me, it was always best as a place to run.

As I start to move again, I remember the reasons I loved it so much.

It is not so much the landscape, though I like the feel of these open moors looking down on the green Derbyshire valleys. Rather, it's something about the process of running here that's its special joy. You have to place your feet carefully, plan your steps between the boulders and the peat—skip up rocks, jump down others, dash through the bogs—and you must do this at speed, for traversing the ground at pace is what gives running its meaning.

As I run over the soft earth, past miles of boulders, I'm conscious of every step and how it feels; I'm conscious too of the irony that, running in such a beautiful place, it's the terrain underfoot that seems to matter most.

I'm also aware that the faster I run, the more attuned I become to the choices, the decisions seeming to flow, each stride leading effortlessly to the next. I find myself thinking of the path as if it were a river: I'm scouting its rapids, adjusting my line, going wrong then putting it right—becoming one with the water. As I reach the main climbing area, I've found a natural rhythm, a balance of speed and awareness that is all that matters.

I notice too that the walkers don't seem to say anything; I am something to be avoided, stood aside from as I pass. It is the climbers who greet me, with nods, waves, the odd shout of encouragement. Perhaps they know something of how, through intense effort, we can transcend the particularity of our situation—those who have climbed for long enough would, I think, recognise what I am talking about.

The miles pass without any sense of effort.

As I start the descent towards Burbage rocks I can see Jane waiting with the car. The last time I ran this route she was here too; on that occasion I would continue, past Burbage and Froggat, Curbar, Gardoms and Birchins edges… to finish after fifteen miles at the Robin Hood Inn. But that was twenty years ago, and though returning is one of my chief delights, I know that some things can never come again.

Aberystwyth

Is there a better town anywhere than Aberystwyth? If there is, I'm not sure I know of it.

In how many places can you park for free, then stroll from the high street to a paddling pool in less than a hundred yards; where shops selling saucy postcards and Welsh rock sit comfortably by upmarket delicatessens, specialist book stores and the ubiquitous New Look; where the cawing of gulls and the smell bladderwrack gives way, as you turn a corner, to grunge music and the whiff of faggots and peas? Then round the next corner, a steam railway takes ramblers to some of the least spoiled countryside in Britain…

You might prefer a trip on the cliff funicular, which ascends to the camera obscura on the top of Constitution Hill. From here you can look down on the castle, or across Cardigan Bay; look west and perhaps you'll spot a dolphin, or north to pick out Snowdon from the pale silhouettes on the horizon.

Aberystwyth is a farming town, fishing port, university hub, centre of culture, seaside resort; home to more winos and weirdos and intellectuals than anywhere I've been. It's like Kathmandu in traditional Welsh costume, and I love it.

I especially loved it today because Dylan had cut his forehead when we were out in the hills. It turns out that Aberystwyth hospital has an A&E department that allows you to park by the door, deals with children quickly and even gives them a teddy for being a brave boy or girl.

And I loved it twenty years ago too.

Because it was here, in a hotel by the sea, that Jane slipped on a pair of blue and white pants and tiptoed to the bathroom, thinking I was sleeping. The wallpaper was brown with orange flowers, the en-suite had royal blue tiles and a fan that clattered—and I told her I loved her.

I meant it more than ever before or ever could again

Genius at work

One of my favourite blogs isn't a proper blog at all. It's the first online publishing of George Orwell's personal journal. Each entry is released exactly seventy years to the day after he wrote it—his life, and the world around him, gradually unfolding. It's an extraordinary read.

For months the diary covered little more than his kitchen garden, recording the progress of flowers, vegetables and chickens. Typically, he'd write: *dug a patch for the leeks, gave liquid manure to the Larkspurs; planted Godetias...* Orwell seems obsessed with his chickens, recording their broody moods, egg production, the amount he sells and at what price. Some days he simply writes: *12 eggs (1 small)*

But in recent months (the daily publishing makes it seem contemporary) he's also recorded the build-up to war. In the entry which follows the one above, he writes with equal calm: *Invasion of Poland began this morning. Warsaw bombed. General mobilization proclaimed in England, ditto in France, plus martial law.*

This is typical of Orwell, recording his mundane chores alongside world changing events, the banality of his domestic life contrasting with profound observation of the wider world. Part of Orwell's genius was to pass comment as if he were an innocent outsider, giving the impression of a naïve wisdom, and tricking us into believing we might have had the same insight.

In fact, the diary is steeped in careful scrutiny. His recording of the coming of war is meticulous; sources noted, newspaper articles appended, due consideration given to other nations besides Britain. Similarly, his garden diary records the seasons and the nature of his district: *Blackberries are ripening... many Finches beginning to flock.*

Seventy years ago last Tuesday, he recorded the British Declaration of War. There's an irony that after following events so diligently he missed the broadcast. I found the transcript on Google, it is worth reading in full, but the extract below illustrates well enough:

We and France are today, in fulfilment of our obligations, going to the aid of Poland... and now that we have resolved to finish it, I know that you will play your part with calmness and courage...

By Thursday, Orwell has returned to his home after travelling to London. He writes, *returning to Wallington after 10 days absence find weeds are terrible. Turnips good & some carrots have now reached a very large size... The last lot of peas did not come to much...*

There is something about the juxtaposition of the two worlds that fascinates and moves me.

Perhaps it's because my life is so far removed from either of their concerns. If I need eggs or carrots, I go to the supermarket; military conflicts are generally distant, experienced through a TV screen or the Internet. The tone of the British Declaration is from a world beyond my comprehension; I can't imagine a general mobilisation, or how I'd feel if my sons were called up to fight. And yet, I know all this happened a mere twenty years before I was born and, more than that, both of Orwell's concerns (food and war) are still the dominant fears in the world today.

Orwell's diaries remind me how lucky I am.

I can't think of a contemporary equivalent to Orwell. At his best, Tim Garton Ash can write with great intelligence and liberalism of thought—but not with Orwell's range or skill. There are others who've written of the same events with the benefit of hindsight and detailed research (Jonathan Glover's *Humanity*, a moral history of the twentieth century is a stunning work that comes to mind), but this is different to writing 'live' and recording the world as it changes around you.

A writing friend once said to me that Orwell gets better with time; it's only now that we realise just how good he was. I agree. Oddly enough, I'm not a huge fan of *1984* and *Animal Farm*; I prefer his essays and documentary writing. His diaries too are fascinating insight into genius at work

The good life

Driving to Wales this morning, Dylan asks me, 'What happens if you work too much Dad?' 'You'd have lots of money, but not enough time to spend it.' 'That's tricky,' he replies. 'I think it's best if you work only enough to be happy.'

Having recently despatched the concept of fairness in a single sentence, Dylan was applying his uncluttered four-year-old mind to the modern dilemma of the work/life balance.

Cash rich: time poor (or sometimes its opposite) is the lament of many middle class households. But the concept of the work/life balance, so beloved of lifestyle gurus, misses the more interesting question of how best to spend the *life* part.

What is it that constitutes the good life in a modern context, and how are we to attain it? It's another of those ponderings that takes up too much of my time.

Plato would have approved; he believed the good life was a one of contemplation, philosophy being the highest form of living. You might argue *he would say that wouldn't he*, but this school of thought is a common thread amongst the ancient thinkers. They were perhaps the first Westerners to record that the quality of life was about more than material gratification.

In the Judeo-Christian tradition which followed, *closeness to God* replaced the idea of the philosopher king, the good life defined by strict moral behaviour leading to spiritual redemption. Friedrich Nietzsche dismissed this as the *morality of slaves*, urging us to find meaning in our lives by pursuing our dreams: *God is dead*, he said; we must find our own salvation.

Nietzsche is a notoriously obscure philosopher with unfortunate fascist connotations, but his prescription that we strive to be an amoral *Ubermensch* is arguably closer to most people's concept of good living than is following the Ten Commandments. I'm not quite there, but I empathise with the idea that we should chase our dreams and that a successful and happy life consists of catching at least some of them.

In a more modern and liberal context, A C Grayling (who would be horrified to be compared to Nietzsche) has written eloquently of how, in the absence of God, we should strive for a life that is richly filled, rather than simply long-lived. Of course, we would like to have both—yet how often do we settle for the sort of comfortable sub-life that wastes time and opportunity. At the recent DO Lectures in Cardiganshire, a range of inspirational speakers gave tips for more productive living; *ditch the TV*, was top of the list.

But surely chasing our secular dreams is only part of the solution. God may well be dead, but we still have a need for something deeper than the *here and now*. Bertrand Russell, in his book *The Conquest of Happiness* said that we need to feel part of the past, and connected to the future.

This seems to me to be right; intuitively we want our children to have a safe and secure childhood, to be loved and feel wanted—we know too, that those who suffer trauma are often disconnected in adult life. Similar claims can be made about nationality, and religion—to deny people their sense of continuity creates a void that no amount of possessions or experience can fill. And as to a connection with the future, children are again our most obvious salvation, but there are other ways to feel we have contributed beyond ourselves—through work, or art, or the example we show to others.

Russell also hit on a very practical idea that I've held to be true ever since I read it as student. He said we need to have at least one interest that we pursue entirely for its own sake—not because it advances us at work, for social climbing or because of pressure to conform, but because we love it in and of itself.

As I write these words I am reminded of the Olympic cyclist, Rebecca Romero, who switched from rowing to track cycling in pursuit of a gold medal. Her victory in Beijing struck me as hollow, as if all that mattered to her was winning; there was no apparent love of the activity itself. I think also of her haunted face on the podium in 2004 (where she won a silver) and compare it to the joy of my kayaking friends last weekend, as they returned from paddling at sea—these are world class performers too, but their motivation is different, and I know which I think is the closer to a good life.

Returning to the 'work' side of the equation, many of these ideas apply equally to our jobs. We want our work to be satisfying; it's a virtue to care about what we do and how we do it. Similarly, a sense of heritage can be an important aspect of our workplace and community identity (think of the shipyards and coal fields; even the recent demise of Woolworth's)—a feeling of future security is equally fundamental to what the management types call 'employee engagement'.

Most of us rightly consider our work at least in part as a means to an end, particularly in the context of the modern limited company, where individual contributions are seldom meaningful in isolation. When just occasionally I see work/life values wildly inverted, the result is a sort of tragedy.

A previous boss of mine was apt to wax lyrical about the importance of family—in practice he came to the office at 6.00am to *avoid the traffic* and seldom left before 8.00pm, supposedly to do the same. In reality, he defined himself by work; *hitting the numbers* was as much a personal challenge as business imperative; by his own admission he saw little of his children growing up and tried to make amends with his grandchildren. Even more tragic, the editor of a newspaper I once worked for, so defined himself by his role, that he committed suicide when he was asked to step aside. We were given the news when he failed to show for his leaving party.

Recently, the psychologist Martin Seligman has written about what he calls authentic happiness. His hypothesis is that we each display a tendency to certain 'virtues'. By virtues he means those character traits that are universally regarded as good by societies everywhere and throughout time—examples include courage, a love of learning, care of others, leadership, creativity, sympathy—in all he identifies over twenty. Seligman claims that the truly happy life is the one in which we have the opportunity to pursue those qualities that are closest to our nature. In my case, I need to find time to think, create, be inspired and develop a deep knowledge of certain subjects—ideally I need do these things with my family and at work too. I know that when I manage this, I feel most happy and motivated; most alive. For others, the recipe will be different, but the concept is the same.

Seligman's ideas take us almost full circle—for it was Aristotle, the student of Plato, who first said that practicing our virtues was the definition of a good life lived. Much though I disliked studying him as a student, I think he was probably right.

But, I'm not so sure that Dylan would agree.

'What makes you most happy?' I asked him as we crossed the bridge at Carmarthen this morning.

'That's easy,' he said. 'It's trains every time.'

Moths

Why would a grown man collect moths?

Why not, I might reply. A less defensive answer would be to say that I don't as much collect them (at least not any more) as I own a collection. This is an important difference. As indeed there are differences between types of lepidopterists.

I suppose your traditional collector is one who spends the dark hours setting up light traps, recording catches and taking selected specimens for their cabinets. They buy gruesome looking equipment from suppliers like Watkins and Doncaster (The Naturalists) and while away the winter hours pinning, setting, labelling and cataloguing their quarry—all the while fretting over the relative merits of British entomological pins verses their longer continental alternatives. I know all about this type of collector, because a few years ago I bought a lot of second hand equipment to... *ahem...* amuse my boys.

Then there are the 'breeders' whose interest lies chiefly in raising live specimens from ova (eggs to the rest of us) through to larvae (caterpillars), then pupae (chrysalis or cocoons) and eventually the imago (adult moth). Sometimes this process takes a few weeks, sometimes years, and it can involve, in various measure, heat lamps, breeding cages and furtive raiding of the neighbour's privet hedges. I know all this too because a few years ago I bought some livestock to,.. *ahem...* amuse the boys.

Believe it or not, there are thriving internet groups who exchange livestock at reasonable prices, sharing equipment and breeding tips. Occasionally I receive urgent email alerts for surplus livestock or rare plants, as some desperate member is losing sleep over his diminishing supplies of *eucalyptus gunnii*. And I know all this because I subscribe to a newsletter which I joined to... ahem... you know what comes next.

(Slight aside here but there is a regular advert in it for a book with the fabulous title of *Fangs For The Memory: Travels of a Tarantula Collector*—it makes me laugh every time.)

So alright, I admit it, I'm interested in moths; butterflies too if you must know.

Quite why, I don't know. Always have been I suppose, though it became more serious when I was about twelve years old. I used to go out at night and watch them circle round the lamps in the streets near our house; I used to go to the Hancock Museum in Newcastle and ask to look at the back room collection; I used to order the larvae of exotic silk moths and rear them to adult specimens and sell the ova to other collectors; and twice I went to London for the amateur entomologists collectors' fair.

I did all this and more—and then I stopped.

In fact, I stopped for nearly thirty years—until my boys were in junior school and they said, 'Do you know where we can get some really big creepy crawlies, Dad?'

That's was why we went back to that same annual exhibition and found it's all still there! The dealers, the collectors, the men with magnifying glasses, the moth trap suppliers, the youngster's bug-club, the stick insect group; the coleopterist group, the exotic livestock group, the photography group—the whole cornucopia of British eccentricity at its best.

We were under strict instructions (ignored) not to bring back anything which was alive. As it was, we managed a selection of caterpillars, and two fierce stick insects that survived for years. Nicknamed Terri and Terrilina, they would attack anyone who tried to go near them. But my prize purchase was a collector's cabinet full of exotic set specimens which cost me £500.

Why did I buy the cabinet?

Because it was there and because I'd always wanted one. And, I suppose, because it reminded me of my youth. A year later I returned and bought a second, which I filled with silk moths—some that I'd kept in boxes since I was a boy.

The collections have no practical purpose. I don't spend hours cataloguing or adding to them. I just like them. Dylan comes to look at 'big blue ones'; visitors occasionally gawp at the twelve inch Atlas Moth—but aside from that they stand untouched by anyone but me. Even I don't look at them often: mostly just to top up the protective naphthalene—*it's an in joke amongst entomologists that the biggest threat to their collections of dead insects is living ones.* I like to think the odour gives my study a Victorian air; Jane tells me it's musty, bordering on creepy. Oh well, each to their own.

And rightly so.

Because it is good to indulge ourselves occasionally. Jane likes clothes; my elder boys prefer gadgets, Dylan is obsessed with trains.... And as for me, I like insects, and lots of other things too. I suppose most collections (or hobbies for that matter) could be regarded as frivolous or nerdy. But I think that misses the point; we enjoy them in themselves, and the best interests give us pleasure beyond any intrinsic worth or purpose.

Despite having looked at thousands of moths, each time I open the cabinet I still get a sense of wonder.

And that, I suppose is, my best answer to the opening question.

Main Wall

Main Wall, 45 Feet—Hard very severe (5b)
Pencilled notes in margin of my climbing Guide
Leader MC, Second KW—cold day, mist
Northumberland—A Rock Climbing Guide

Bowden Doors is a sandstone outcrop on Belford Moor, east of the Cheviots in the Scottish Borders. In my twenties it was the place of my dreams; the place I learned to climb and where I came of age. It's a place that has never left me. And so I find it astonishing to think that this picture was taken 25 years ago.

The route had obsessed me for years—almost since I began climbing.

Main Wall: the name said everything—no nonsense, just an obvious line up the centre of the crag; hard, steep, uncompromising. And appropriate to the bitter winds and big skies of Northumberland's moors.

I'd known for some time that I was good enough to climb it. But I wanted to do it in style and many times refused to practice on a top rope. The route took on a significance well beyond its grade, beyond most other things in my life—climbing it was about more than just moves on rock. By December I had been putting it off for months—for far too long, in fact.

I remember fragments of the day. Ken perched on a ledge taking photos; Simon and Katie flirting and not very interested. The rock, dry and sharp, the smell of it muted by the cold. There was mist that day too, a pale blue fret that the sun burned slowly away. By early afternoon the crag was warmed with a golden light.

I walked over and uncoiled the rope.

In the picture I'm at the crux move, a high step to leave the corner and pull onto the blank wall. I'm heading for the pinkish scoop about four feet above me—there's a tiny nubbin that appears as a dark brown dot half way between my body and the scoop. I'll transfer both hands to this and step up, my right foot smearing on a thin groove.

I know all this because there are certain climbs that stay with you: the easy first moves, the awkward balancing in the corner, the dry mouth, the wall above. And I remember the sharpness of the grit as it bit into my fingers—the tension in my tendons as they held my weight.

And the joy as I made it!

I remember too the snug placement of a nut, to save me should I fall—and stepping onto the upper wall, all difficulty behind me—powering upward—jug holds for my hands, and the rest of my life ahead of me...

Post script

Although this post is reminiscence, I had returned to Bowden Doors the year before writing it—a pilgrimage of sorts. My father was dying and I'd travelled north to see him, the first time in twenty years. That evening I drove to Wooler and the next day returned to the crag where I'd sought to escape.

There was a young boy struggling on the same route.

'You reach for the nubbin,' I said. 'Place your right foot high, and pull for all your life...'

When I die, I'd like my ashes to be scattered there.

Thoughts on food and sex

My blog today was going to be about food, but pondering what to write my mind drifted back to one of the first writing courses I attended...

It was more of a retreat than a course. We were sitting in the common room, a group of twelve students and a tutor-cum-facilitator. The wine was open and we'd exchanged pleasantries. What plans did we have, our tutor asked?

There came the usual replies.

One lady was writing prose poems in memory of her son; another was finishing the second volume of her historic trilogy; a doctor from Leicester was writing a farce about the Health Service—a *consultant had been caught pissing in the sink; his gay lover, who chaired the disciplinary panel, was being bribed by a nurse with Münchhausen's Syndrome who was slowly...*

Everyone laughed and I was nervous of explaining my modest goals. But as I came to speak, I was interrupted by a stout lady with a thick German accent.

'I am coming here to write about the sex.'

There was a short pause in the chatter.

'How interesting,' the tutor replied. 'Feminism is such a challenging subject.'

A longer pause.

'I am not wanting these woman issues. I am wanting the sex.'

There followed a chink of wine glasses on the coffee table; eyes to ceiling, windows, floor...

'I'm sorry, I don't quite understand?' the tutor continued.

'It is simple; I am only liking the fucking.'

The silence which followed is one of the great comedy moments of my lifetime. It's beyond my powers to describe the excruciating discomfort of those present. Eventually an elderly lady piped up.

'Might I say, isn't that a bit pornographic. I mean, sex in its wider context is one thing, and passion as part the range human emotions goes as far back as Shakespeare... '

'No, I am only wanting the sex.'

By now I was holding my sides and the doctor from Leicester was frantically taking notes.

The German lady went on to make a serious point. She wanted, she said, to write about sex, and specifically the sexual act. What's more she wanted to write about it directly, not by use of context, euphemism or symbolism. This was difficult and most writers bottle out.

She continued:

'It is like in writing about the cooking. The chefs... they write about the history and the region and the preparations... but I want to know about the food. I want to know how it is tasting. I want to know what it makes my mouth feel. This is what we need with the writing about the sex is it not?'

By the end of her speech our tutor had recovered her composure. 'That sounds very challenging,' she jollied along. 'Particularity is one of the essentials of good writing. I'm sure we'll all be very interested to hear how you get on.'

And we were too.

Each evening a few students would read from the work they'd written that day. The doctor made us laugh with his farce, there were nods of sympathy for the prose poems, and suitably constructive feedback on the second volume of the trilogy.

Sometimes the whole group would gather, more often it was just a few. But there was a full house the night our German friend was due to read. Wine glasses were quickly filled as she opened her folder to speak...

'I have not been doing very much the fucking. So I read you about my favourite meal instead!'

There was an audible sigh.

Of relief or disappointment, I couldn't quite say.

A very human prison

I seldom bother with newspapers, but today my assistant showed me an article in *The Guardian* that I read three times.

The story described the ordeal of Rom Houben, a student who was paralysed in a car crash and misdiagnosed as being in a permanent vegetative state. More than 23 years later his doctors discovered he was fully conscious—trapped and screaming at a world that couldn't hear.

Houben's condition reminded me of the journalist, Jean Bauby, a victim of Locked-in Syndrome, who eventually wrote of his experiences by 'blinking' out the letters of the alphabet. His book, *The Diving Bell and the Butterfly*, was a bestseller and later became a film. But at least Bauby was able to communicate in some way—he wasn't thought to be 'extinct', the description applied to Houben by his doctor.

In reading the article I kept trying to work out if there was an analogy to the 'brain in a vat' idea—was it a kind of equal and opposite condition I wondered?

It isn't. The 'brain in a vat' hypothesis suggests that we could all be captive minds, controlled by electric impulses that simulate reality (as in the film, *The Matrix*), and yet we wouldn't know it.

But Houben was not a brain in a vat and there was nothing artificially stimulating his senses. He knew exactly what was happening to him and why. It's astonishing that, in such circumstances, he didn't go insane.

Houben's solitary incarceration brought to mind Brian Keenan's haunting memoir, *An Evil Cradling*, to my thinking the best account of those taken hostage in Beirut. In it, Keenan describes his four-year imprisonment by terrorists, much of it in isolation. But his ordeal is not comparable either; he could move and converse and elicit a response, albeit trapped in attrocious conditions.

Ultimately, the closest analogy I could think of was those patients who've reported full consciousness under anaesthesia. They describe their helplessness as the doctors operate on their body. Houben didn't have this pain, but he suffered something of the same terror for 23 years.

Our horror at these stories is understandable. But I find the idea of Houben's situation particularly shocking. And I think this says something about what we consider most important in being human. Ultimately it is our minds that most differentiate us and give us our place in the world. A fully functioning brain trapped in a paralysed body is somehow the worst form of imprisonment.

Consider the opposite situation to Houben's—though it's quite hard to conceive—one in which the mind is paralysed but the body fully active. This is what we might call the Zombie scenario; a being that we don't consider 'alive' in the normal sense. The underlying folklore is that without the mind we are 'living dead'.

From an ethical standpoint, it's often our minds—and our capacity for complex thought—that causes us to value human life over that of other animals. Anything less, says the philosopher Peter Singer, would be speciesism, making an analogy to racism and sexism. The primary reason, he claims, that human life is more valuable than other forms, is our ability to understand our existential situation; to have a sense of the past and aspirations for the future.

But to have that capacity, and yet be unable to enact it; to have all the reception but none of the transmission, is a deeply sobering thought. Is there any price, I wondered, that we might put on our agency? Brains in vats—or indeed, Zombies in palaces—are all well and good as 'thought experiments', but would any of—really and truly—want to disconnect the messy mix of our lives and our minds for something less than our own?

I was thinking all of this as I went for a run this evening; smiling at the rain on my cheeks, the wind bending trees and my calves burning as I turned for home and a blog post to write.

Roosting

Near my house in Wales is a starling roost. As many as a million birds return each winter's evening, many of them travelling more than thirty miles to rest overnight in a copse of fir trees on the south side of Plumstone mountain. The squadrons arrive in waves, forming dense clouds that swirl and twist above the trees—not dissimilar to those Attenborough films of fishes balling and coiling in defence against dolphins.

It's breath taking to watch.

But why do they do this?

Some say it is for security. Other claim it's for warmth, or to pass on knowledge of feeding grounds. Yet none of these explanations seems sufficient.

Why travel so far and expend so much energy? Why gather in such a large group, only to leave as individual squadrons at dawn? And why run the gauntlet of the raptors, waiting patiently on telegraph poles or soaring above the trees to pick off the stragglers—last night, they were dive bombing the murmuration in the hope of randomly striking a kill?

We can hypothesise their reasons but, in truth, we don't know.

Perhaps they simply have an instinct to return; like salmon coming back to spawn and butterflies migrating across continents.

Or like me, travelling to Wales—seeking a sanctuary that seems always worth the effort, logical or not.

Windsor Chair

As I sit and type this post my arse is getting cold, and somewhat numb too. The chair it's attached to (save for a thin layer of cotton) is a Windsor stick back, made of oak, by someone a long time gone. If I turned it over I could show you the marks where they've drilled and chiselled so the legs butt neatly in the slab.

I found this chair almost thirty years ago, in a shop in Monmouth, shortly after coming to Wales. It was one of those impulse purchases—saw it; loved it; bought it—and at £190 it seemed a lot of money at the time. I remember too that it caused a row because my wife was annoyed I'd not asked her first. *It's my money* I'd said; *and it's our house,* she'd replied—to be fair, she had a point.

It was always my chair after that, and when we parted, it came with me too. There are few days since that I haven't settled in its frame to ponder or write. A while back, my company insisted on supplying me with an orthopaedic monstrosity, complete with lumbar support and variable height adjusters—it soon adorned my shed, before making its way to the tip.

Stick chairs are traditional, vernacular furniture—they were common throughout the UK, but particularly so in Wales. Experts can identify the region of origin, sometimes the maker, and ironically, for what started as humble country effects, they're now sought after antiques with provenance and prices to match. Some of the designs (Windsors particularly) have been adopted by manufacturers, and you'll find any number of reproductions on eBay.

But despite the mass producers, stick chairs are still made by craftsmen today. The twentieth century guru was John Brown, who published a definitive book on styles and method. His chairs are objects of beauty; among the few things I truly covet. There are contemporary makers too—so it's a craft that lives on, though more for sales than for personal use.

By today's prices, my £190 wasn't a bad investment. More importantly, it's given me three decades of pleasure and memory. The surface of my chair is pitted with history, a palimpsest of my time in Wales. That's the character of the possessions we care for—objectively, they are 'worth' this or that—but what's the value of the wear on the arms, the chips in the varnish, the nicks and scratches that make up our lives?

As I finish this post I can barely feel my backside. I ought to get a cushion; indeed, probably will—but it's a familiar discomfort, and I wouldn't want to have plonked it anywhere else.

Interlude:
Why blog?

Why bother blogging?

That's the question I'm most often asked by writers with a sneaking interest in the form's possibilities, but an intangible reluctance to commit.

The short answer is, that if you take blogging seriously, it will make you a better and more professional writer. The slightly longer one is perhaps best explained by a brief diversion.

Julia Cameron (author of the bestselling *The Artists Way*) is widely regarded the guru of 'morning pages', a practice of writing freely for up to 30 minutes each day, connecting hand to brain in a way that flexes its creative potential. Her book, *The Right to Write* is especially excellent; I practiced morning pages for two years when I first took up writing and in many ways regret that I grew out of the habit.

Not entirely dissimilar is the practice of journaling—a form of extended diary keeping that typically includes creative reflections, poems, the drafting of ideas; shopping lists if you wish. I've never been a regular journal writer and am mindful of straying off my patch; I'm also fully aware that journaling is so much more than the crude summary I've given. What matters though, is that a great many writers find journaling and its sibling, diary keeping, a helpful and even slightly addictive form—for some, it's the main focus of their work.

But why talk of these practices when my subject is blogging?

The reason is that they have a superficial similarity which means they are often confused: the comments that most often follow *why blog* are 'What's the difference between a blog and diary?' or 'But I already write a journal.'

To some extent the confusion arises because of the etymological origins of the term. The word 'blog' is derived from 'weblog', a label coined the 90s to describe a regular record of incidents on the Internet.

This in turn gave rise to the idea of blogging as a form of shared record, with obvious similarity to diaries, journaling and their derivatives. There's an abundanceof information on this subject, scholarly articles even, if you care to look. It's interesting too.

But to return to my theme… I'd suggest the underlying concern of the questions above is essentially, 'Why bother putting it all online—what, specifically, does bloggingachieve?'

Which gets us to the heart of the matter…

Blogging is public; it's a form of *publication*.

And that's the longer answer in nutshell.

I could extend it by saying that as a consequence blogging demands a level of attention and care for your words for which no amount of private journaling, diaries or morning pages can ever be substitute. We might also talk about the myriad of possibilities and connections which follow from that singular difference… but we'll come to all that in soon.

For now, some writers reading this may decide that what I've said is good enough reason not to start. And I'd respect that choice, because blogging isn't for everyone. But if you have something to say and you want your words read by others—not just yourself or a self-selected few—then I'd suggest blogging is one of the best, the easiest and, perhaps surprisingly for a solitary pursuit, the most supportive ways to go about it.

In a moment, I will move my cursor over the orange arrow to the right of the screen and click to publish this article—that twitch of my finger will not only share but also transform what I've written, sparking connections that bring the words truly to life.

That's why you should blog as writer—in a sense, everything else is fluff.

Painted Lady

I know precisely when I saw my first Painted Lady: the 19th of August 1974, in the garden of my Aunt Marjorie's house.

Marjorie wasn't my real aunt. She was our primary school nurse and friend of my mother. Her husband had died in India, serving as the batman to Lord Hunt, who led the first successful Everest expedition. She was a redoubtable lady whose house was stuffed with eastern artefacts and Catholic icons; she drove a red Ford Capri with a casual disregard of the Highway Code, seldom bothering to change gear.

Looking back, I realise that Marjorie's house was a place of escape for my mother. At the depths of my father's depression, we would go there from school. And I'd be sent to the garden, my mother explaining they had 'things to talk about'. Marjorie would give me a jam jar and tell me to hunt for caterpillars. 'Don't get lost,' she'd joke, 'it's a wilderness out there you know.'

And she wasn't exaggerating.

Her garden lawn was as tall as meadow grass, the borders overgrown with foxgloves, convolvulus, and climbing nasturtiums. There were patches of stinging nettles and thistles, a forgotten bed of lavender and sedums growing between torch lilies that we called Red Hot Pokers. And most impressive of all, by the rear fence, were three towering buddleias, large enough for a small boy to hide in. Two of them bloomed purple madder; the other pure white.

The wilderness was Marjorie's delight, her decadent secret in contrast to the clipped roses and crazy paving out front. It was also, though I didn't know at the time, a perfect butterfly garden. And it was there, sitting beneath the buddleia with the *Observers' Book of Butterflies* that I learned to recognise my first species; red admirals, tortoiseshells, brimstones, large whites and peacocks.

After I left primary school, we stopped going to Marjorie's. She retired the year I left for the grammar, by which time my mother had learned to drive and found new freedoms. I was making my own escapes too and might well have forgotten about my mum's elderly friend.

Except occasionally, especially when the sun was out, I'd cycle by her house and pretend to be passing. We'd stroll down the garden, inspect the nasturtiums and observe what was feeding on the buddleia. I kept records in a little pocket book that I still have. And I remember her excitement at the Painted Lady.

'They come from Morocco,' she said, explaining how her husband used to say they were pilgrims. 'How lucky one should be here on your birthday.'

Puppet Daddy

When my older boys were small I bought them each a cone puppet. They were from Paris, very expensive; the sort of toys that parents like. The boys thought they were spooky, and perhaps because they played so much together, they didn't feel a need to involve other characters. The puppets languished in a cupboard for a decade.

Dylan discovered them when he was three. Next to trains I'd say they are his favourite toys, especially Puppet Daddy, who, Dylan insists, is controlled by me. This is interesting, because to Dylan the whole point of the game is to talk to the puppets rather than handle them.

Puppet Daddy speaks with a screeching Welsh lilt, modelled on Norma Price from *Fireman Sam*—Dylan won't let me change it. *But he's a boy*, I say.

He's a puppet Daddy, Dylan corrects me.

He's a nervous one too, retreating often to his cone, especially at any sign of his nemesis, Boppy Jester. Boppy speaks incredibly fast and plays the singular role of bashing Daddy on the head at any opportunity.

And so the game goes on.

Except Puppet Daddy's great sadness was that he had 'no legs'. This regularly caused him, and Dylan, to cry. He couldn't go to school, or escape his enemies, or play football; he was confined to his cone and hours in the dark.

Perhaps he could hop on his stick? I once suggested.

You can't hop without legs... said Dylan.

Tears flowed.

Until, that is, Dylan found some plastic boots from an Action Man. *Puppet Daddy's legs*, he cried, *I've found his legs... go and tell him; go tell him now!*

And so, Puppet Daddy has limbs of a sort. He remains nervous, of course. After all, he is only learning to walk—and Boppy Jester is still to be avoided. But great was the joy the day those tiny boots were found.

And great joy we have had together since: the mornings I've been woken with, *Will you be Puppet Daddy now;* the ongoing saga of Boppy Jester (*don't find HIS legs Daddy—he'd be too boppy*); the surreal time Puppet Daddy accompanied us to Wales and I spent the weekend talking in a high pitched woman's voice; the videos we've made, the cuddles, the laughs, the insanity of it all…

Almost every parent can tell you of a time they bought some expensive gift only for their little darling to pay more attention to the cardboard box. I know very little about the psychology of play, but I suspect there's something important in allowing children to transcend themselves. The problem with so many of the branded toys, is that they're based on formulaic characters that limit possibilities and contain the imagination.

Toys like Puppet Daddy are different. They're about invention and sympathy and absolutely believing in and living with every turn and detail of the tale.

Nobody could design Puppet Daddy, he just was, and is. In a few short years he's grown into a complex, lovable, irreplaceable person.

And as Dylan sneaked into my bed with him this morning, I realised how much toys can imitate life.

Moments of transcendence

Last week I called in to see my artist neighbour, John Knapp Fisher. He's one of the finest painters in Wales , working from the small village of Croesgoch on the North Pembrokeshire coast. On the walls of his house-come-gallery was a tiny water-colour of a bare field, the furrows white with snow, trees stark against a bitter sky. It was dated 1962; the sticker said, Not For Sale.

I was living in Suffolk when I painted that, he told me. *I gave it to my father and when he died, I had it reframed.* I reminded John that I owned a similar picture that I'd bought off him twenty years ago. *I did a number that year,* he replied. *But you know, I remember everything about this one: the smell of the field, the trees bending, the taste of paint on my lips. I remember the brush strokes, the colour of my water—everything, everything,* he said again.

I smiled as John talked. His words said more about the intensity and integrity of the picture than could any formal description. I knew too, something of what he was saying.

On my computer is a photograph of Daniel and Michael when they were small. They are lying together on a double bed—the visitor's bed, we used to call it—where they would often choose to sleep together. I remember thinking they looked like figures by Klimt. And I remember too, the smell of that room, the warmth of their breath as I kissed them and pulled the covers over their soft bodies. I recall Michael stirring, and me standing for minutes, watching them from the half-open door. I remember dimming the light, the sound of the TV, and the taste of salt on my lips as I walked downstairs.

I suspect we all have experiences like this. Moments when, for whatever reason, and perhaps for only an instant, we see things differently. Moments that burn into our consciousness, unlike the billions of others that we'll never recall.

A few months ago I watched an interview of the scientist,

Buckminster Fuller. He was talking about a girl in a white dress that he'd noticed walking off a ship, fifty years previously. *I don't suppose she even saw me*, he said; *and yet not a day of my life has passed without me thinking of her.* Why was that he wondered, and what did it say about human memory and consciousness?

The truth is I can barely remember the details of my sons being born, and yet if I think of climbs I did in my twenties, I can bring to mind the shape and sequence of each hold, the pull on my fingers, the strands of heather on the ledges... And more darkly, I have images from my childhood, of a father with manic depression and little self-control, that have haunted me for forty years.

The artist Terry Frost said that his painting could take that long to gestate. In his later life he was painting the fields and boats and sunsets he had seen as young man. The late Pembrokeshire painter Peter Daniels said something similar to me once; *I'm interested in the moment of seeing; the instant before consciousness; before we categorise and commit the image to memory.*

Talking to John last week reminded me of this. It reminded me too of how art—be it images, music, or writing—is a means of connecting with a world beyond ourselves. And how when that happens, even in some small measure—even in a photo of two sleeping boys—it can bring back memories that are more vivid and real than the taste of the coffee I have just put down.

Coming of age

I have a picture of myself taken on my eighteenth birthday. It isn't the best likeness (not sure that smile was quite mine) but it's the only one I have. It was taken by my girlfriend; before we went to university, before our first jobs, before we were married and later divorced. It was also taken before I learned to climb, before I cycled in the Pyrenees, before breaking my leg and buggering my back. It was taken before coming to Wales, before meeting Jane, before the promotions and house moves, before my children… I could so easily fill this page.

I have a vivid memory from my early teens of deciding that life didn't properly start until you were eighteen. Lying in bed, I'd count the months I had to endure—calculating what percentage that was of the 'sub-life' I was living. Reaching eighteen was about as far ahead as I could imagine (though back then, the idea of being twenty one still held some additional significance). I doubt if I ever calculated the months to reaching thirty; that was as good as infinity. My 'proper life' would stretch on for ever… if only, that is, it would hurry up and get started.

And yet somehow tomorrow is my fiftieth birthday—and that picture taken by my girlfriend seems at once a day and an age away.

Shorty after it was taken, I left home. I spent three years as a student and have long regarded that as the period I truly grew up. But thinking now, what about my first job, my first house—all the things I listed above—aren't those times just as significant? I hope never to stop learning, never to stop facing the new or seeing the world differently—and in that sense, never to stop coming of age.

I was given a birthday card this week—it proclaimed fifty was the new forty; some wag even suggested 'thirty'.

I hope it's not.

Because for one thing, the older I get the more comfortable I've become, not so much materially or even physically (though my waistline's certainly more relaxed these days), but in my own skin; in my sense of being me and being confident with what that means. Youth has its delights but it also has its uncertainties and pressures. In my case it was dominated by anxiety and a sense of being deeply alone. It took me another eighteen years to admit that to anyone.

And so being fifty doesn't seem that bad. It feels to me (and allowing for a few ups and downs) that life's getting better, not worse. Despite what we read in the news, I'd argue that's true for most of us, there's more freedom in the world, better health, information, nutrition, education.. just about everything bar pensions and intrusive wind-farms (sorry, couldn't resist and don't want to get too serious).

When I said this to a friend the other day they replied, *but wouldn't you like to be eighteen again, except with all you have now?*

Leaving aside the impossibility of the wish, I'm not sure I would, for it devalues the journey. Sure, I'd like to live longer; I'd love to be fitter and wish I still had my hair... But I wouldn't gamble what I've had for another chance at life. I look at my children, at Jane, at where I live... and I feel extraordinarily privileged.

With a little luck and grace, there'll be more to come.

A pocket book of flowers

Author's note—this post has been one of those wonderful serendipities of blogging. Years after writing it I still regularly receive emails and comments; someone once wrote to say their grandfather had been Macgregor Skene, the author; others write just to say they own and treasure the same book.

I went to my local car boot on Sunday. *How much for the little green book?* I asked a trader. He wanted a quid; I offered fifty pence and we agreed to split the difference.

What I'd bought was a pocket book of flowers—or more accurately *A Flower Book For The Pocket*, by *Macgregor Skene, Professor of Botany at the University of Bristol.* It's one of those beautifully illustrated field guides that became popular in the Forties as printing techniques allowed for cheaper reproduction of colour plates. The book is quite scholarly by today's standards, though it's written with real skill which makes the taxonomy accessible to the layman, a style that was later perfected by the Wayside and Woodland series and their ubiquitous cousins, the Observer's Books.

This particular copy was bought in 1943 and it cost someone ten and six. I know that because there's a price mark on the first page and an inscription that reads:

To E from W.

When WE went NW.

August 43.

E has written her name, E M McGarry, on the inside leaf. I suppose E could just as easily be a 'him', but the writing looks feminine so I'm going to presume otherwise, not that it matters.

Whoever E was, she was a diligent botanist, ticking and dating the illustrations, noting any variance to the description. Common Hemp-nettle, she observes, is taller than described and Hedge Woundwort has solid not hollow suckers. She's added details of flowers and variants not included the book, commented on the accuracy of the illustrations, and my favourite, noted that 'high heathland' would be better defined as 'heights over 1500 feet'.

In '44 E saw a Hemp Nettle at St Brides Major (all her dates use an apostrophe). That same year she recorded a Marsh Gentian in Norfolk, Knotgrass in Cornwall and Water Avens at Borrowdale. Between '43 and '45 she includes sightings from Cambridge, Dartmoor, Stonehenge as well as Salisbury, Ogmore, Cowbridge, Exmoor and Suffolk. On a few occasions she's picked flowers and pressed them between the pages, their impressions still there after sixty years.

Reading her notes, it's possible to create a fictional portrait of E.

From the frequency of the place names I'd say she came from the West Country, and she must have had transport to travel so far and so frequently. Remember, all this took place during the Forties, so presumably she was well off, and by the look of things, well-educated too—her handwriting is beautifully formed and the accuracy of her notes indicates more than a keen amateur. As for who W was—her companion on that trip to the North West—a lover perhaps, or a sister?

I adore these old books, and to me they are enhanced by the notes and jottings of a past life. I have a copy of the *Wayside Book of Dragonflies* that includes handwritten lists of species seen in Wiltshire over many years, there is even copies of the previous owner's correspondence with the book's author.

To a collector, books that have been marked are often devalued, the descriptions on eBay will typically say *'some scribblings and notes throughout'* or *'considerable wear and pencil markings'*. What they don't say is, the book includes a life that took joy from nature; someone, who in the midst of a world war, stopped to list the flowers she saw.

Those recordings stop abruptly in 1947.

What happened to E after that I wondered? The notes gave me no clues. Until that is, I turned to page 353, almost the last of the book. And there, in that same handwriting, though this time in biro, was the underlining and ticking of Bladder Sedge, with the note *Bratton Fleming '97*.

I like to think that E lived a long life, that she had many books like this—that perhaps she turned to an old copy to remember W and reminisce about those trips to the Lake District and Cornwall. Bratton Fleming is on the edge of Exmoor—not quite 1500 feet above sea level.

I wonder if she's buried there, and what flowers grow on her grave.

Route finding on Snowdon

On Friday, when half the nation was watching 'that wedding' I walked up Snowdon. It wasn't so much an act of protest as an opportunity to climb a great mountain on a fabulous day. Hundreds, possibly thousands of others, had the same idea.

Snowdon (*Wyddfa*) is the highest UK mountain south of Scotland. The massif consists of three distinct peaks, arranged in a horseshoe formation, but it's the central summit that most climbers aspire to. From its trig point are some of the most spectacular views in the UK. It was fifteen years since I'd last stood there.

My route took me up the old Miners Path, returning by a variant known as the Pyg track. Both are now scars on the mountain; their routes passing the industrial detritus of a lost age, as well as the disgraceful hydroelectric pipes that are today's equivalent. On the final slopes is an incongruous and yet somehow not inappropriate funicular railway line, and to top it all is a dull, box-like, cafe. It must be one of the ugliest mountain tops in wales.

Snowdon then, is magnificently flawed. It has sweeping views and hidden corners that leave me breathless, yet within yards there's as much that brings me to rage; huge tracts are untouched wilderness, a small proportion so tramped that the rock steps need replacing. It reminds me of what a colleague said about Wales when I first came here, *the ugliest and most beautiful place on earth*.

Friday had its share of diversity too. I passed a man travelling barefoot, another in a ceremonial kilt; there was a woman wearing an ankle length black hessian dress and matching hijab (her husband wasn't burdened with this inappropriate garb). Finally there was even a couple carrying golf clubs to play pitch and put on the summit.

Actually, that finally isn't correct. For there were hundreds more walkers in fleeces, families in shorts, lads in hoodies and girls in not much but tattoos. There were Welsh and English and Japanese and

Dutch and Eastern Europeans and Americans… A toddler was having a strop because she wanted the picnic *now*; a chap who looked at least ninety was swaying in the wind—I was worried that if he stopped he wouldn't start again.

And yet amongst all this it was someone else who came to mind.

Almost thirty years ago, on the day that Prince Charles and Diana Spencer were married, I walked with my grandfather up Windy Gyle in the Cheviot hills. It was the last proper mountain we'd climb together. I remember us arriving at the summit cairn to find a group of about half a dozen disaffected blokes all smoking pipes, *you've escaped as well*, they said.

We saw an adder on our way down and I recall my grandfather explaining how to use the intersection of the horizon as guide to your height on the mountain. I showed him where I'd camped when walking the Pennine Way and how I'd found water in a hidden gully. We had a shared love of the landscape that transcended other differences; obvious ones like age, but also attitudes to politics and ways of seeing the world. He was scientist; I'm… well at that time I was probably all of a muddle.

And it was walks like those that helped me become a little less so.

Twelve years later, when my grandfather died and soon after I first climbed Snowdon, I asked for his compass; it couldn't be found. No matter, for in a sense I'd already inherited it.

They say we don't change much beyond our teenage years, at least not in our personalities. It's the experiences we have as young people, what we are given and what is taken away, which fundamentally shapes our inner self. And thereafter, no amount of life's wear and tear can make much difference.

I'm not sure if that's scientifically correct. But sheltering under Snowdon's trig point on Friday, it felt about right. And as I looked across its scarred slopes, over my half-adopted country, towards the north and east, to the land of *my* father, it felt as true of this place as it was of my granddad, and ultimately me.

Red Admiral

Sunday morning at midday and I'm sitting in the car with drizzle spotting the windows when what should land on the wipers but a red admiral. It's possibly the last 'on the wing' butterfly I'll see this year—there will be some that hibernate in my shed and of course there'll be chrysalises too, but neither of these are quite the same.

The red admiral is for me one of the quintessential English butterflies. Its arrival in Northumbria, where I lived as a boy, marked the start of summer holidays. Along with peacocks, tortoiseshells and painted ladys they would feed on the Buddleia bushes in our avenue and we'd try to catch them with nets made from bamboo poles and old lace curtains. They're a butterfly that makes you stop and admire (*it was for a long period erroneously named the red admirable*), even allotment gardeners don't chase them away.

In fact, the species is not really English at all—it's a migrant that rarely survives even our milder winters—after last year's cold snap it's doubtful the one I saw came from anywhere other than the continent. I suppose it could be a second brood—some of the early arrivals breed in spring, their larvae forming web nests on stinging nettles. But the emergent adults then have to face the winter, a few choose to fly south.

I read the other day that in Welsh their common name is *y fachtell*, which I think means *the cloak*. With its black and red forewings, I've often thought the butterfly has a vampire look—so perhaps the day before Halloween was an appropriate time to see one. In the event, it drank only from my windscreen.

This year has been poor for butterflies and moths, but the warmer autumn has given a late surge and as always, there are exceptions—the hummingbird hawk moth had a bumper year. A migrant too, over 11,000 were recorded this summer. The other week on the coast path, I saw dozens of small coppers, a delight of colour in the October sun. And I saw a painted lady on our anniversary, the only one this year.

Next time you see a red admiral, consider its journey and think again about how robust these deceptively delicate creatures are. Alternatively, you could smile at the answer a pal once gave in our secondary school quiz. *What's a red admiral?* was the question. To which he replied, *It's an Indian sailor, sir.*

Given that some of them come from almost as far, he wasn't entirely wrong.

Missing Lives

This post was an almost incidental review of a book about the aftermath of a war that we'd too quickly put aside as 'past history'. Reading it again, at the height of the conflict in Ukraine, I'm struck by how events so tragically repeat themselves and in doing so give writing fresh relevance and even an unintended prescience

I'm suffering from a bad night's sleep; my restlessness made worse by the knowledge that I have to get on with the day. But you'd be wrong in jumping to the conclusion of 'one too many whiskeys'—it's way more complicated than that.

In fact, it was words that sparked my insomnia; words and pictures to be more precise. For last night I stayed up reading *Missing Lives*, a new book by Nick Danziger and Rory MacLean. It recounts the atrocities of the Yugoslav wars, and its disturbing power is that it does so, not by historical essay, but by telling human stories, so simple as to be beyond misinterpretation.

Missing Lives is the stories of bereaved families searching for answers. It is the stories of survivors as much as victims: survivors and victims of the ethnic cleansing, the teenage conscription, the religious bigotry, the political manipulation, the fear and the barbarity—survivors and victims of a conflict which claimed over 140,000 lives. Yet fifteen years after the Dayton Accord, nearly a quarter of those who died are still unaccounted for.

I have long thought that, to West European eyes, the Yugoslavian war was an unfathomable conflict. Most of us barely knew the location of the emerging countries let alone the towns and regions and subtle differences between the various quasi-nationalist factions.

MacLean's words and Danziger's photographs transcend that complexity, focusing instead on the intuitively understandable anguish of its aftermath. And by telling much the same story from each and every side—Muslims, Christians, Bosnians, Serbs, farmers, judges, parents, orphans—they make it clear there were no winners and eloquently emphasise the pointlessness as well as the brutality of it all.

For when you think about it, the Yugoslav conflict was a particularly horrific war. So much so that the philosopher Jonathan Glover described it as being amongst the worst atrocities of the Twentieth

Century. His reason is that it happened so late in the century, at a time when the protagonists ought to have known better and have learned from the past; when communication was such that we in the 'West' knew what was happening (remember those TV reports from Srebrenica and Sarajevo) in contrast to say, the sketchy knowledge we had of the regimes of Stalin or Mao in the Fifties and Sixties.

Thinking back, I recall my own feelings being that it all seemed such a long way off. Somehow those strange sounding names—*Srebenica, Kranska Gorja Banja Luka*—gave it a distance that was greater than the geography. Not only that, but the whole religious and nationalist aspect was based on history I didn't understand. Even when British troops were part of the peace-keeping forces, I don't think I understood who or what we were keeping apart. And I suspect I was better informed than most.

If my feelings were typical—and I suspect they were—it is not only a sad indictment of our media, it also says something about our isolationist attitudes. The writer Tim Garton Ash has argued that the Yugoslav wars would never have happened in the European Union—partly because of the political structures, partly because of the shared values and history of 'Western Europe'. The conflict, he argues, (together with other conflicts that followed the break up of the Communist Block) is perhaps the best demonstration of why the European Union should be cherished—and why it is so much more than the bureaucratic laughing stock the media delight in portraying.

For the disturbing truth is that the war was marked by its proximity rather than its distance. To think it took place just over the border from Austria is something worth reflecting on. So too is the shamefully slow response of most European states. Though we often knock the hypocrisy of American foreign policy, it was the US that made the decisive interventions on what were largely humanitarian rather than political grounds.

To me the most disturbing aspect is another sort of proximity: how close each of us might be, in similar circumstances, to losing our humanity; how little it takes for 'ordinary people' to tip over into barbarism. Fear and propaganda no doubt fuel that transition. I'd like to think in our comfortable democracy we have better and deeper values.

And yet, somehow I doubt it. The people whose stories are told in *Missing Lives* are much the same as you and me; so too are may who acquiesced or even perpetrated unspeakable horrors. As I lay awake last night I kept thinking of football matches I have been to: the chanting, the tribal behaviour, the nearness to violence—if more were at stake than three championship points I'm not so confident of our better side winning out.

Missing Lives is a collection of stories, each astonishing and horrifying in itself; stories which, according to MacLean and Danziger, need to be told. It's also a sharp reminder of how lucky we are and how fragile is so much that we take for granted. And that's the unnerving thought, which gave me the sleepless night.

The importance of scale

Although for many years I was a committed a painter it's been a long time since I saw works that made me want to pick up my brushes. Much of the art in commercial galleries seems little more than fancy decoration, and frankly, I've lost interest in looking. My loft is full of canvasses that I can't be bothered to hang.

So how refreshing to be metaphorically hit in the solar plexus by the artist Julian Meredith. Giving a talk about his work he said, *Reduced scale images are part of the reason why we now ignore them*. And I felt that long forgotten rush of adrenaline (yes that's right) as the photographs of his life-size image of a blue whale hit my nervous system.

Meredith's comments about scale are wise. Size is a fundamental quality of any artwork, impacting on its meaning and context, its ability to connect with our senses. We've become used to paintings and sculpture that reduce our experience—and they do so more than just physically. The other week, I went to the Leonardo exhibition at the National Gallery, possibly the most over-hyped show this century—I don't want to be churlish about his art (oh for a morsel of that talent) but the vast majority of pictures were tiny; even the showpieces could have hung in my hall. Ultimately we 'peered' at the work—mostly over dozens of heads, all jostling for a better view.

The whale prints were so large they were made in sections that bordered on the abstract, and as such had an individual quality that goes beyond the whole. They were woodcuts, and I liked it that he's used an elm that was felled at Alnwick in Northumberland, near where I used to live. The choice of elm—a tree almost entirely lost in the UK—to make an image of one of the rarest and most endangered animals seemed especially apposite. So too, that they were hung at the Natural History Museum as a temporary replacement for the fibreglass model that is one of its iconic exhibits.

In fact the prints were quite small for Meredith's work. On his various residencies he has created sand sculptures, earth works in chalk and stone (he described the Cerne Giant and Uffington White Horse as two of our greatest works of art), including a 400 foot white whale near Cardiff. His works are so immense that it's possible to become fascinated by how he makes them. But as he so rightly pointed out, (he was almost irritatingly insightful) we should be careful about the value we place on process—it is the image that matters.

That said, everyone at the lecture was taken aback by his descriptions of print making directly from fish and swans—dipping their bodies in ink and pressing directly onto paper. In answer to a questioner, he explained that one swan might suffice for eight to twelve images—and no, he didn't kill them himself but used donated specimens.

Julian Meredith is the first visual artist in many years to truly spark my imagination. It's curious that I've always been interested in both very small and very large works of art. By the end of my 'painting career', I was working simultaneously on postcards and pictures that were fifteen feet long—unsellable images that I would sleep besides, so that on waking, they'd fill my eyes. I'd not thought of them in years, but last week I realised I'd soon have some time on my hands…

End of day fish

My grandmother used to display glass fish in a cocktail cabinet; next to frosted whiskey glasses and souvenirs from seaside holidays. There were figurines from Spain (though she'd never been) and a resin cast of two hands holding a book inscribed with a poem titled *Mother*. At the bottom of the cabinet were two drawers of assorted 'treasures'—I remember a half packet of cigarettes marked with the date she'd smoked her last.

I adored my paternal grandparents. My grandfather was blind and crippled with arthritis; my grandmother stricken with 'nerves' and, until she gave up, constantly puffing on Embassy Virginia. They'd lived through two wars, the great depression, and even seen Newcastle win the FA Cup: a generation gap that's almost unknown today. But for all they were of a different era, they could sense enough of our world to know things weren't right at home. As a teenager I'd cycle to their house on a Saturday—or midweek in the holidays—and they'd be complicit in the secret when I visited again with my parents on Sunday mornings.

So my grandparents' house was a place of refuge—emotionally and sometimes physically. And you know, I think that's why I like glass fish—they remind me of that cocktail cabinet, and how important that place was to my childhood. I can't think of another reason. For glass fish are rather ugly, most of them of the same designs; they're seldom worth more than a tenner and sell at car boots for pence.

Yet I have boxes of them.

To be honest, most of them are in the loft and it's some time since I payed for any or was given one as a gift. People used to do that when we first bought our house in Wales; that was the height of my fish collecting phase. And it's probably not coincidental that my grandfather used to say he dreamed of living in a cottage, of being close to nature, even if he did see it in idealised terms and would have quickly missed his Wallsend council house. Our cottage had a Fifties feel to it then, so I suppose the fish fitted the decor too.

But there's another connection—and I've never told anyone this. I once broke one of my grandmother's fishes.

As I waited for a belt round the ear she picked up the shards, rearranged the figurines and gave me a hug—*never mind* she said, *there's more treasures in the drawers*. That behaviour would be nothing special now; but at the time it was to me astonishing, and I remember lying awake and thinking how I might find her a replacement.

I never did do that. Though I still have two fish on display in my cottage. They're made of the speckled glass that is known as '*end of day*', after the practice of using up the last of the molten pot to create unusual objects at the end of a shift. Later it became a general term for designs that were flecked with colour, the result of rolling glass specks into a clear mixture. I suppose I like the idea that many of these are improvised pieces; I like too their unpretentiousness and to some extent the way they border on kitsch.

I doubt I'll collect any more fish—and frankly the ones in the loft ought to be eBayed for charity. But I'll always keep a few. And just this week I took another one down, to place in a bookcase, next to some worthless yet priceless treasures of my own.

A matter of faith

The first book of popular philosophy I read was Bertrand Russell's, *Why I am not a Christian*. It's still in print and remains one of the best summaries of why we should reject religious dogma. Russell's contemporary equivalents—Dawkins, Hitchens, Grayling—are all writing in his shadow.

Not that they should be ignored. Richard Dawkins' *The God Delusion* is an exemplar of applied logic and ought, in my view, to be a standard text of any critical reasoning syllabus. Christopher Hitchen's *God Is Not Great* would be a strong contender for additional reading; his litany of the inhumane consequences of religion is as breathtaking as it is horrifying.

It therefore, won't surprise you to learn I'm an atheist and have been since I read Russell's essay at the age of eighteen. I've never flirted with agnosticism because I'm not a fence-sitter, and in any case, it's largely atheism in disguise. For all my adult life I've held to this view and not been so much as mildly persuaded there's any evidence to the contrary.

Yet for all this, I've always been fascinated by some of the great themes of religion: *what constitutes the good life, what gives it meaning, and how should we best treat others?* Much of the philosophy I studied was concerned with ethics and justice—not a far cry from the central concerns of many creeds. I share with many religions a reverence for the natural world and can feel awed at the enormity, the inexplicably of it all. In a way, I'd like to be religious; to discover answers to these ultimate questions; to have a sense of purpose and a belief system that is simpler and more reassuring than the vagaries of Humanism.

The problem is, I can't bring myself to overlook what I see as religion's conflict with everyday reason. The literal beliefs of all the great monotheistic faiths strike me as ludicrous and the modern interpretive versions as equally unconvincing and at times rather desperate attempts to maintain belief. On the subject of which, I can't accept that 'faith' is in any way compatible with, or an acceptable alternative to, the logic we expect and exercise in almost every other aspect of our lives. I am in short, a post-Darwin rationalist.

I have other misgivings too, in particular the exalted status we give to religion in society. Last week's judgement that town councils should not begin their working sessions with prayers seems to me to be entirely right (imagine if we did this at the office). I have profound misgivings about the teaching of Biblical stories in primary school and I cannot agree that religious education should be taught in a way that disavows criticism. Contemporary wisdom is that all beliefs should be respected—imagine taking that approach to physics! I could go on, but none of these are matters of faith.

It would also risk the impression that I'm hoping to convert you to my stance, which is truly not my aim. Rather I'm trying to explain why I feel as I do. To put into words why, when I see the Alpha Course advertised at our local church, I rail at its claim to be a genuine enquiry. To declare my incredulity at a friend who recently explained she'd not read *The God Delusion* because her faith made it irrelevant. To shed light on why, try as I might, I find it so difficult to understand those who are comfortable with inconsistency of beliefs.

And yet…

A high percentage of the most interesting, caring, humanitarian people I know are religious. Many of my friends are either committed or deeply curious in matters of faith—our discussions are always challenging and engaging; I admire them for their enquiry if not their conclusions and certainly respect that they are seeking answers just as I always have. What's more, I find their value set almost invariably closer to mine than those of my secular acquaintances. For all Hitchens and Dawkins bemoan the historical consequences of religions, when you bring it down to an individual level it's seldom threatening. In general— fundamentalists and strident evangelicals aside—I rather like people who have faith.

What's more, the vast majority of my religious friends are highly intelligent—people who in other aspects of life are an inspiration and influence on my views. What is it, I often wonder, they see that I don't? What am I missing? I may have held my views since reading Russell's essay, but if they could only help me here, I'd be delighted to change.

Perhaps surprisingly, it is their very faith which is my primary chink of doubt on the entire God question.

Except, of course, the imperfections of our personal logic, especially when applied by our self-interested and inadequate intellects. I'm well aware that the goal of objectivity is more of a dream than a realisable state. At its most slippery, rationality becomes rhetoric.

But for all this, I can't shake the conviction that reason is the best we have—to be applied by each of us, to the best of our ability, with humanity and generosity, but without compromise. Bertrand Russell was a long way from flawless, but the essence of his message remains true to me, and has shaped my thinking—albeit imperfectly—for all of my adult life.

Shrew

The other day I saw a shrew. It was a fleeting glimpse and such a tiny creature—*which leads me to think that maybe it was a pygmy shrew*—that, had I blinked, I'd have missed it. At the time I didn't give it much thought, but afterwards, I began to consider the sighting more carefully.

I can't remember when I last saw one and, to be honest, I'm not absolutely certain I'd seen a shrew in the wild before. I suppose I must have—I recognised it instantly, and shrews are relatively widespread mammals aren't they? But if you asked me to pinpoint when or where, I'd be a bit stumped. Before last week, it's just possible I'd only seen pictures of them in books.

This shrew in question was in Colby Gardens in Pembrokeshire, snuffling for worms under a sheet of galvanised metal that I happened to lift up. In a way, it was lucky I came along because the sheets are placed to attract snakes which would happily accept a shrew-sized meal. Last spring, lifting the same sheet, I found the most gorgeous grass snake, chocolate brown with a golden band like a collar around its neck—not that snakes have necks as such. When I disturbed it, the snake slid unhurriedly into the surrounding meadow, reluctant to leave its warm den.

But last week's shrew took a more panicked flight, scurrying to an escape tunnel and wiggling its bum in a last goodbye. An extraordinary little thing, I thought, ludicrous in its way; like a tiny vole with Pinocchio's nose.

Next moment it was gone.

I'd always thought shrews were a type of mouse, but evidently, they're more closely related to moles. And like those, they are fiercely territorial, only coming together to mate. They have the greatest ratio of brain to body size of any mammal, including humans—and they need to consume their own body weight in grubs every day. One web site I came across, claimed that if a shrew doesn't eat for two hours it will die. *I presume the author means if it goes longer than two hours between meals rather than actually eating for two hours!* And some species have venomous teeth, which no doubt the author of that website would wish me to experience for being so darn pedantic.

It occurred to me that most of our wildlife encounters are fleeting, especially of mammals. I'd guess the popularity of bird watching is at least in part because most of them will actually allow for a decent viewing. In contrast, I remember Jane lifting a flagstone in our garden and finding a nest of baby dormice—so as not to disturb them we replaced it immediately. As such, my lifetime's total of dormice watching is three seconds! Last year I saw my first polecat in years: five seconds. And then there was that weasel which ran across the road as I was driving…

It turns out that encountering a shrew is quite rare after all. They may be commonplace (pygmy shrews less so) but field sightings are definitely not. You need to be in the right place at the right time. And if you're lucky enough for that to happen—then, unlike the shrew, which is virtually blind and relies on sounds and smell—try not to blink

Clear September sky

The path from Whitesands to Abereiddy traces one of the longest unbroken stretches of the North Pembrokeshire Coast. For nine miles there's no access by car and, with the exception of the smugglers' cove at Pwll Caeorg, the cliffs maintain their height throughout. At this time of year, Atlantic grey seals come here to pup. It's the inaccessibility of the rock beaches they favour, seemingly untroubled by the storms that scour the granite and slate of all but barnacles.

Jane and I walked their yesterday. We saw the first seals at Porth Lleog, barely two hundred yards after our leaving the car; they were two females, lolling on their backs in the sunlit surf. It was one of those breezy mornings, a jade sea, spotted with the shadows of scurrying clouds; bright one minute, showers the next.

To the west of Carn Llidi is a hidden valley of ancient stones and feral ponies. It shortcuts St David's Head and leads to the sheltered cove of Gesail Fawr, which my minimal Welsh translates as the *big armpit!* Here we saw our first pups, four of them sleeping on the rocks, their mothers basking in the clear water under the hundred foot cliffs. Two of the pups looked newborn, a third so plump its features had lost all definition; the fourth, older again, had fur that was mottling from cream to grey.

By now the sun had chased away the showers and the breeze was at our backs. We made good progress toward Penberry, passing a few walkers on a sponsored hack. There were gulls and rock pigeons on the cliffs, a great skua floating in one of the bays—and on the landside, the last of the wheatears, their little 'white-arses' (their old country name) flashing across the field stubble.

Beyond Penberry, we watched a kestrel hovering over the bracken. They are surprisingly scarce in Pembrokeshire, their inland territories lost to buzzards and kites—one birder told me the increasing numbers of goshawks played a part too. But they thrive at the coast and I often see them at the Head or the Porthgain quarries near my house. Of all birds of prey, I think kestrels are my favourite; they remind me of my blind grandfather, his gnarled hands holding mine as we'd walk each other to the scrub fields by his house. Windhovers he used to call them.

Beyond Penberry the path had been strimmed and I wondered aloud if it was a way of managing the wild flowers. Probably not, but it seemed plausible. As the sun warmed the bracken some butterflies came out: a small copper, a common blue, three tortoiseshells. I was telling Jane that it's been a poor year for butterflies, the numbers in the national count down by 11%. 'You know,' I said, 'I haven't seen a painted lady all summer' two years ago, there were thousands passing here on a mass migration.' No sooner had I stopped talking than one opened its wings on the rocks by my feet, its auburn wings edged with scales of black mascara. That alone would alone have made my day.

There was a seal pup at Pwll Caerog too. We didn't realise at first, mistaking it for a rock in the stream that trickles to the pebbles. A young couple on the beach pointed it out. They were camping at the bunkhouse they said, but they had to dash because their friend was getting married in an hour—on the campsite above the cliffs.

Jane and I were married twenty years ago this week—we were meant to go to Rome but work intervened. Instead, we came here, eating flapjacks and drinking tap water from a plastic bottle as we listened to the pup's mother calling in the bay.

At Abereiddy we bought mugs of tea from the van that is always there. The storms of a fortnight ago had carried thousands of rocks to the lip of the breakwater; the beach, normally black with shale, was a glistening ochre. 'Give me a kiss,' said Jane, 'and don't you dare pull away.' The surf was spoiling in the wind and I could hear the jackdaws reeling above Blue Lagoon quarry.

When I opened my eyes, the pools of an ebbing tide were bright in a clear September sky.

Interlude:
Starting out

There was once a time when launching a blog was oh so innocent: when you signed up and simply started typing; when there were no concerns over branding or monetising or content creators pitching search engine strategies…

In those days blogging was as easy—and almost as natural—as teenagers walking on a beach, hand in hand, the salt on their lips as they plucked up courage for that first…

Okay, it was never quite like that.

But it was certainly easier to make a start back then. The abundance of considerations that we have today simply weren't around, and while I don't want to stretch my metaphor or romanticise halcyon days (in my case that beach was cold, it was probably raining and a kiss wasn't always forthcoming), the lack of complications had its advantages.

Blogging has always been pretty simple—and over-thinking our first steps risks what the marketeers call 'analysis paralysis'. That very phrase hints at the kind of concerns whichI want to avoid, for they will quickly distract us from what matters. Despite all the advances that have come with time and technology, the core decisions are much the same as they were back then: which platform to choose, what audience to reach, and most importantly, what and how am I going to write?

I'm not going to cover all the technical detail, because thankfully I don't need to. The leading platforms are all a doddle to set up and if you've any queries the help sections on their web pages will be more up to date than anything I could write here. I'll touch on some other routes you might go, but for now let's dive into the two options that the vast majority of bloggers choose from.

Blogger and WordPress are as divided in their followings as surely as Catholics and Protestants, and yet like those two traditions the underlying hopes and convictions are much the same.

Blogger has the reputation for being the simpler of the two—it's less flashy than WordPress, is owned by Google and about as plain and simple to navigate as their homepage. You sign up and literally within minutes you're the author of a blog that looks professional, is accessible worldwide and part of a network that gives you access to an audience and like-minded writers. As its name implies, Blogger is designed specifically for bloggers. *Views from the Bike Shed* is hosted there and if it's now a little hick and old fashioned, well, I quite like that.

WordPress is marginally less intuitive and the more technically minded users often host their blogs separately to the free version's servers. It's part of the open source movement (which is appealing to some) and has an almost endless array of templates and plug-ins. WordPress is also the world's leading website platform and as a result the distinction—not least in appearance—between a blog and website is more blurred. Already, you may have picked up a sense that more 'serious bloggers' tend to opt to use WordPress.

Is that true—and does it matter?

Frankly, I think not. I'm sure there are armies of fans for either platform who'd say otherwise, but I'm persuaded in these matters by friend Michelle, who's the first blogger I befriended online and who, in one of life's most serendipitous of moments, just happened to live a mile from my house!

Michelle began by writing a blog about her allotment—which, now that she's given up her plot, has evolved into the broader theme of gardening and horticulture. She writes with joy, experiments with ideas, and engages her audience with a passion for plants and a homely humour. As a result, she's won several awards, contributes to journals and magazines, has an enviable press-pass for the Chelsea flower show, and an international following who share in the shoots and seasons of her suburban pottering.

And she's taught me a lot.

Before compiling this book I wrote to her asking if she'd ever migrated a blog from Blogger to WordPress—perhaps it was time that I did so?

Her reply was typically pithy. Why would I want to do that? What was it that WordPress offered which Blogger couldn't provide? What feature was I hoping to gain? She reminded me that my blog was about my words; that I was first and foremost a writer and that hadn't changed—or had it?

And she's bang on the money.

I've not transferred *Views from the Bike Shed* to WordPress because—the mild irony of this book aside—there's no need for any other platform. Fourteen years since I first signed up, Blogger provides all I require and most importantly, it's a means not an end to publishing my work.

There may come a time when this changes, and I understand, especially for many of the young people I've taught that their blogging can have different objectives; that an awareness of formats and more technical matters might open up career opportunities; that a professionally presented blog can be a compelling and real time CV.

In other words, I can see that blogging for writers, isn't just for writers like me.

But what I do believe—passionately so—is that blogging as a writer should be about your words not the platform, or the pictures, or the fancy pants distractions that it's all too easy to be seduced by.

Sure, there are well known authors with dedicated web pages and integrated blogs—set one up in that style if you wish. And there are travel blogger and lifestyle blogger and sports bloggers... many of which have developed brands that they nurture. None of this is to be excluded; all of this is possible down the line—but it should come with time and good reason not at the expense of what you have to say.

Which is why the third option is worth looking at too.

For while I have reservations about Medium there are more than a hundred and fifty million users and it has the advantage of avoiding the need for any set up at all. If you don't know what Medium is, then search it out—in short, it's an online publishing platform that mixes professional and amateur writing and, by offering the potential for payment in return for readership 'claps', blurs the lines in-between.

Blogging on Medium gives you a username and a profile—you can post pretty much whatever you like and you have access (as both reader and writer) to interest groups and 'publications', offering the possibility of an audience that few personal blogs could ever hope to achieve.

The reality, however, is somewhat different to the hype—vast amounts of submissions languish unread (to be fair, the same is true of Blogger and WordPress and all the other platforms I've not even mentioned), to fully participate requires a subscription, and—how shall I put this tactfully?—so many of the articles look and read the same.

Medium feels to me like the world epicentre of posts titled 'five ways to boost your brand' or 'ten tips for mental wellbeing'—writing that's little more than marketing copy dressed up as insight. That's a touch harsh, for there's quality there too, but I sense the payment model of Medium drives the over production of neo-click bait that's often as fake as it is forgettable.

The other consideration is that Medium doesn't give you your own webspace—essentially, you're posting on their platform. Conversely, I often see writers promoting, 'my article published on Medium' as if that's more than perhaps it is. Which reminds me that Medium feels quite American—just that bit brasher than maybe I'm comfortable with.

There are other hosting platforms too and by the time this book is published there will no doubt be more. Substack is a sort of cross over between blogging and newsletters with a subscription element for followers; then there's Wix and Squarespace and Joomla…

But you see, here I am going down rabbit holes when they really aren't necessary.

The essence of what I'm saying is that you should simply choose an option, sign up and start!

That's truly the best advice I can give.

It takes minutes to do and it's actually quite fun. Once you've set up your account, write some posts, add a picture or two if you wish… then click that button and… you're published writer!

Of course, it's not quite that simple—you now need people to read what you've written; you will want to experiment; you must find what works for you and for them… And there's a whole world of blogging to explore—from the great to the dreadful, the joyous to the dour; the mountains to the sea…

But the critical thing is that you've taken your first step.

And like that kiss on the beach we began with—had a taste of how things might be.

The passing and turning of wheels

Albert Winstanley is dead, and so is Alan Oakley. I'd bet very few readers will have registered the former (Albert died this March), and while you might have heard the news about Alan, I doubt you knew his name before today.

Alan Oakley was the chap who designed the Chopper bicycle: the best selling bike that Raleigh ever made. It was a Seventies icon that saved the business and wrought havoc to the testicles of 20,000 teenage boys. I was never allowed a Chopper—they were for 'bad lads', my father used to say—and my pleas that it would be good for the paper round made no difference. Instead, he got me a 20 year old three-speed roadster which weighed a tonne and was laughed at the first time I rode it to school.

Albert was from a previous generation, and a writer, not a designer. He rode a touring bike with a cotton duck saddlebag, a rolled cape strapped on top; the old photos show him in brogues and baggy shorts, about as far from the street-cred of Chopper riders as it's possible to imagine. Albert had toured across Europe when most folk were still heading to Blackpool for holidays—but he was best known for his forays in the North of England. In the unassuming columns of the Cycling Weekly and Cycling World his recollections of *golden days awheel* captured a delight in the outdoors that was keenly felt by many of the post-war generation.

I was 25 before I could afford a decent touring bike. That hadn't stopped me cycling and camping as a kid, or riding the hundred mile round trip to see my girlfriend when I was at university. My most vivid cycling memory is riding in Leicestershire through fields of oil seed rape. It was a new crop back then and I remember marvelling at the acid lemon landscape—and feeling more free and less troubled than ever before. I still love rape fields; I know they've replaced swathes of pastoral countryside, but I can't help it—every time I see them, I remember that day.

This evening, in the park near my house, a group of teenage lads were skulking under hoodies and baseball caps. They came to sit by the bowling green, some way from the club house but near enough to provoke discomfort. 'Here's trouble,' said one of the members as the bowlers finished their twenty-first end. In the event, nothing much transpired; a bit of swearing, the odd kick to a litter bin… Jane was annoyed they'd spoiled the peace; I couldn't help it too, even though I know it's only youthful rebellion. They soon departed, two of them on stripped down BMX bikes—the modern equivalent of a Chopper.

It's stretching things to say that cycling has defined my life. But it's been a constant presence and, in many ways, my bikes, and the joys they've given me, mirror my journey too. There's a part of me that will always wish I'd had a Raleigh Chopper—that wanted to be one of the 'bad lads'—and another that knows they were never for me.

Just as there's a part of me that's delighted to see the thousands of new enthusiasts riding cyclo-sportives each weekend… And another, that thinks they should travel more like Albert—with a saddlebag and rolled-up cape—through fields and fells that would harvest memories of golden days awheel.

Because it's there

Because it's there, is the line attributed to George Mallory, answering the question of why he wanted to climb Mount Everest. It's probably the best known summary of what drives mountaineers.

That's understandable because the quote is a memorable and witty encapsulation of an urge that's beyond the comprehension of some. It also works at a deeper level, in hinting at the sense of adventure, the pull on our imaginations which mountains evoke.

A strong candidate for the opposite of Mallory's line is the quip I must have heard a thousand times while climbing—*there's a path round the back you know*! Not only is this not witty, it hints at a lack of originality in the joker who called it out.

I'm being unfair in that last paragraph, for while it's easy to dismiss the wags, it's more difficult to answer their underlying question—*why are you risking so much on something so intrinsically pointless?* The problem with the Mallory quote is not that it's wrong, but that it's incomplete. The motivations for climbing are many and complex, and no soundbite is ever going to be a credible answer.

Alfred Wainwright said that we climb mountains, not for the view from the top, but from below. I understand his point—climbing a mountain changes our perception of the landscape. We look differently at the peaks we've climbed—we have association, familiarity, a shared history.

There are other reasons too: for bravado, for status and pride (at national and personal levels); popular at present is raising money for, and awareness of, good causes. The recent proliferation of adventure sports draws on these and many similar motivations.

But as explanations, they remain incomplete.

For in my view, tackling all but the most casual of mountains, involves an inner as well as an outward journey.

It's well understood that the hardest routes require as much composure as physical strength. But 'control to power' is not what I'm getting at. Rather, it's the counter-intuitive fact, that by being so physically all-consuming, climbing gives us a space to reflect and rejoice—to feel more alive—that's so difficult to find in our daily lives. At its best climbing helps us come to terms with the world and our place in it.

In a sense, we climb not because *it's there*—but because *we are*.

Straight Life

The title of Art Pepper's biography is loaded and layered with meaning. 'Straight Life' is the name of his best known composition, a virtuoso piece from one of the greats of twentieth century jazz. But the tune was always a contradiction, for Pepper's body was wracked with addiction: his reasoning twisted by alcohol and heroin, and his life-path as crooked and fucked-up as they come.

Art was arguably the greatest alto saxophonist of the post-war era. Born unwanted, brought-up unloved, the descriptions of his childhood are as grim as they are shocking. There can be little doubt that his later problems stemmed from a deeply rooted sense of isolation—a craving to be loved and accepted, by himself as much as anyone else.

What followed was a life story that's staggeringly sad. In an echo of his music, it's as if Pepper was improvising on his own desperate existence: playing ever faster, increasingly off-key, out of sync with himself and the world. Ostensibly he was seeking redemption—but always, and inevitably, his actions resolved into a deeper and more pitiful hell.

At one level *Straight Life* is a chronicle of self-destruction, of time spent in and out of prison, of failed relationships, petty and serious crime; it's the story of years wasted, in more ways than one—the consequence of a willful surrender to substance abuse.

At another, it's a troubling reminder of the fine line between brilliance and the void.

Pepper's life is a tale of obsession, of an uncompromising (if seriously warped) view of the world and what constitutes right and wrong. By any normal standards he's an odious individual; the nagging question is whether normal standards should apply.

The book's format is a transcription of recorded interviews which he gave towards the end of his life. In Pepper's voice, there's a disarming honesty and a declared self-criticism, but there's also a less than subtle suggestion that his actions were a necessary consequence of his talent.

My suspicion is that fans of Pepper will sympathise. We often lionise our heroes, tempering our judgements and blind-eyeing actions that would be unacceptable in others. Art Pepper was as near to genius on the saxophone as they come. Whether that excuses behaviour we wouldn't wish on or from ourselves, is a different matter.

Pepper, like his music, is difficult and mercurial—it takes time to figure him out. The book is much the same, and there's a quality to *Straight Life* that took me a while to grasp. Throughout the narrative, Pepper talks entirely 'in the moment' of his recollections. When he describes entering San Quentin prison, it's as if he's back there and his attitudes and opinions of the time are expressed as if he still held them now—by the end of the chapter they've evolved and moderated, but only as the tale unfolds. It's as if each moment has to be fully relived—a sort of method acting as a means to honesty.

And perhaps that's what's required of great jazz musicians—the ability to live in the moment; achieving a creative dissonance that suspends reality; a sort of nirvana if you like. I don't know if that's true, but it seems plausible and might explain the link between his destructive qualities and musical talent—the flowering of good and evil, each from the same root.

Straight Life is not an easy read. It's complex, self-indulgent and, frankly, depressing. But there are moments of lucidity that make it worthwhile. The passage describing his first hit of heroin is a piece of brilliance—it's too long to quote in full, but here's an extract to finish on.

I looked at myself in the mirror and looked at Sheila and I looked at the few remaining lines of heroin and I took the dollar bill and I horned the rest of them down. I said, "This is it. This is the only answer for me. If this is what it takes, then this is what I'm going to do, whatever dues I have to pay..."

Art Pepper died in 1982; his music lives on.

Karnali river

I came across a photograph when sorting the contents of my study. The figure in the centre is me paddling a rapid named *Sweetness and Light* on the Karnali river. It was taken in April 1993.

The Karnali is the biggest river in Nepal; it lies in the far west of the country, running steeply from Tibet, through dense forest, toward the Indian plain. At that time, the river was a recent discovery for kayakers. My friend Phil Blain had been on the first descent, an audacious self-supported expedition—our trip was one of the first to use rafts and take 'paying customers'—we calculated that less than fifty Westerners had been to the area.

When I think back, the risks we took astonish me. For a start, I was not that good a kayaker; I had been to the Alps a couple of times and paddled a bit in the UK, but to make the leap to Nepal would never be recommended today. The Karnali was also extremely remote (*there's now a road*)—access required a long trek over unmapped mountains, porters, self-sufficient supplies; there were no satellite phones—and we had no expedition doctor.

This minor omission nearly proved fatal.

We arrived at the river on a late afternoon, setting up camp on a beach surrounded by trees, monkeys screeching in the canopy. The porters inflated a raft and, as the sun was setting, I helped them carry it to the water. With my first step into the silted river, I felt a grinding tear in my foot—the water ran red and I fainted.

The porters carried me to the camp, blood pouring from the wound. I'd stepped on a flint, cutting deep to the bone, across the width of my instep. I remember lying on the sand and the faces above me, the grimaced smiles; *you'll be fine,* they said, *only a cut.* Their voices betrayed the lie, though strangely I didn't feel any pain—in fact, I couldn't feel my foot at all.

My friends cleaned the gash with neat iodine, stitching it crudely after practicing on the skin of an orange. Four of them held my legs as the needle drew the flesh together; Jane gripped my hands. When it was over, she stayed with me as the others huddled out of earshot. The porters were asked to wait overnight; I was given some rum.

The next morning, before the others woke, I crawled to my boat. It took me ten minutes to launch it, shuffling inch by inch towards the water. I paddled across the current, capsizing as I hit an eddy but rolling upright without problem. It convinced me that the damaged foot made little difference to my paddling.

When I returned I noticed the porters sizing me up. One held a large basket, big enough to carry a man; they'd fashioned holes for legs and makeshift straps to hold the passenger steady.

In the event, my fear of being carried over the mountains was greater than facing the river. I insisted we send the porters home and my friends reluctantly agreed. Jane sat with me as the rafts and kayaks were prepared; the river our only option now—it would be ten days before we reached a road.

As it turned out, the problem was not so much paddling the river as scouting the lines. Because I couldn't walk, I had to rely on sketches drawn in the sand. With waves the size of buses these proved useless. I was effectively running the river blind, chasing the tails of other boats and praying they'd chosen the safest line.

One time I got it wrong, ploughing headlong into a deep recirculating wave. I was sucked deep into the current, emerging shaken but breathing downstream; my boat followed five minutes later—bent like a taco by the power of the water. After that I ran the 'chicken shoots' on the bigger rapids: easier lines that give relatively safe passage through the maelstrom.

By the third day, my foot was too large for anything but a sandal. After a week it had doubled in size. We had no antibiotics, the wound was drying but my leg was swelling. Thankfully, the river eased and we could make faster progress. By skipping a rest day we made it to the road in seven or eight days.

Back in Kathmandu, I went to the Canadian hospital. There were mice running across the floor of the surgery. The doctor was horrified, but not at the vermin. He gave me strong antibiotics and told me I'd been a fool to refuse the carry-out—either that or I'd been in shock. Probably, it was a bit of both. The expedition had taken a year to organize, I'd come half way across the world; I wasn't going home without trying.

Looking back, I have a certain pride in my decision to see it through; at the very least it's a good pub story. But in truth it was as much to do with fear as any macho heroics. Continuing also taught me something of my weaknesses. Regardless of the injury, I learned I was not as confident as I'd hoped in such extreme environments; that Jane, who had *come for a ride on the raft*, was essential to my sense of security; that I had survived rather than conquered the river.

Eighteen years later, as I sit in my study flicking through old photographs, I can still feel the scar on my foot. I remember too, the speed of the water, the screams of the monkeys; the bridge at Chisipani as, at last, we reached the road.

And, on balance, I think that's a good, if imperfect, outcome.

Papillons de nuit

As boys, my brother and I would go hunting for moths. We used homemade nets and would roam the avenues by our house, lurking under street lamps and looking for tell-tale flickers. The moths would gather around midnight, and we'd make our way to the railway station, where the bulkhead lights cast a glow over beds of nettles and convolvulus.

You'd never see that now: two boys in duffle coats, walking the streets with nets and jars. But I'm glad I was allowed, because for me it began a fascination with travelling at night that I love still. There's a tension to moving in the dark, an alertness that's akin to what nocturnal prey must feel—for though it was me that was hunting the moths, I've always felt more like the hunted.

Perhaps that's why we caught so few. But we did learn a lot about their behaviour: how they spiralled, which ones would fall to the ground, what conditions were best and when not to go at all. In August there'd be hundreds of yellow underwings. Once we caught an elephant hawkmoth, and we discovered the larvae of the willow hawkmoth nocturnally feeding in the trees of Belsay Gardens. We even smeared rum-laced treacle on the trees to see what would be feeding next morning.

There are 800 species of larger moths in the UK, about 2,400 if you include the 'micros'—this compares to about 50 butterflies, and explains why most lepidopterists soon turn to the night. And you'd be wrong if you thought moths were all dull and brown—indeed, the bigger ones are more spectacular than butterflies—*papillons de nuit* the French call them, and they're right. They are right on another level too, for there's no absolute distinction from butterflies—taxonomically, they are all of one lineage.

By the time I was a teenager I had a moth trap—its actinic tube emitted an ultraviolet glow that would attract hundreds more than a street lamp. It's not the brightness to our eyes that matters, but the colour on the light spectrum. Have you noticed there are much fewer moths around lampposts these days? That's because most street lamps are now yellow, one of the least phototactic colours to insects. You'll see more moths in your headlights than you would by walking the streets.

In my mid-teens I started to make money from my interest. I'd buy eggs of exotic silk moths (*Saturniidae*), feed the larvae, store the cocoons and breed the adults in cages I made from net curtains—then sell the hundreds more eggs at a profit. Forty years later, I still receive newsletters from the Exotic Entomology Group—*and as an aside, if anyone's thinking of rearing some caterpillars with their kids, silk-moths are way easier and more spectacular than butterflies.* I bought my boys some moon moth cocoons when they were toddlers—I remember them crouching by the cage, awestruck and whispering, as the adults emerged and their pale wings filled with fluid, expanding to a six-inch span, the long tails twisting below.

Moths are possibly the most ignored of the major creatures we could easily observe. Most of us get a thrill in recognising wild mammals—birding is hugely popular; plants and trees (*okay, not creatures, but you know what I mean*) too. There are more beetles than moths but the identification is tortuous and frankly they are hard to find—similar problems apply to spiders, wasps and ants. Yet in most gardens, you could almost certainly record a hundred *papillons de nuit*; they'd be there most of the year too, feeding and breeding and flying to your window—butterflies of the night.

Passing thoughts

This week I learned of two deaths—they could not have been more different.

On Tuesday I was told that my former father in law had died. He must have been ninety or thereabouts; a kind man, gentle, with a wry sense of humour. I'd not seen him since I separated from my first wife nearly thirty years ago, but I'm grateful still, for the care and support he gave me when starting out on adult life. I hope the fact that we didn't speak says as much about distance and life moving on as any lasting anger on his part.

When I heard of his passing I didn't shed tears. Death at any age is sad, but there's comfort in the knowledge of a life well-lived. We can celebrate what the person gave us, rejoice in shared memory, and—especially if there are descendants—take comfort in their contribution to the greater life journey.

For my part, this is as close to faith as I get.

Yesterday I also learned of the death of one of my son's best friends. More accurately, I should say 'had confirmed' for we knew both through the grapevine, and in our hearts, that the skier reported to have fallen 650 feet in Oz-en-Oizans, was Jordan.

One slip on the ice and…

As I write these few words, my fingers are tensing at the keyboard; my eyes are wet and it hurts to swallow. I'm thinking of the time he came to our house and we played table tennis in the garden—so vital, so competitive, such fun to be with… Twenty years of the life force embodied in physical form.

And because of that, and because he was such a good friend to my son, I feel anger as much as grief. Anger at an industry that pretends the mountains are a helter-skelter ride; which revels in putative adventure but diminishes the risks. Its apologists will cry otherwise, but they are wrong… and the litany of deaths every year gives evidence to their self-deceit. There's more to be said on this, much more… but now is not the time.

Every night this week I have slept badly; troubled in a way by my own distress. After all, Jordan was my son's friend, not mine; I'd met him only a handful of times. I know that in part, it's a dread of 'what might have been'; a parental unease at events that feel too close for comfort—'but for the grace…' as they say.

But there's more to my sadness than that.

For if I'm honest with myself, the first line of this piece isn't strictly true. To a man of no faith, all death is the same—oblivion—regardless of when and how it occurs. That void is beyond our knowing, and as such, I can just about bear it. What's harder to reconcile, are the memories cut short, the potential lost—the link to life's journey, more severed than stitched.

That will take time to pass.

Monocular

Two days ago, at the summit of Pen y Fan, I reached into my rucksack and took out a small leather pouch. Inside was an old Russian monocular which magnifies at a paltry 8x30; the lens was dirty and the focusing wheel so stiff it required two hands to turn. I've no certainty of the make (Zenith possibly?) but its serial number is 8011162, and oddly, I've known that by heart for thirty-seven years.

I bought the monocular when I was coming up nineteen. It was my first summer as a student and, in between signing on, I spent it backpacking the long distance paths of Northern England. I couldn't afford a proper case so made the pouch myself, hand stitching the brass zip into the mock suede fabric. That long July and August it came with me on Hadrian's Wall, the Pennine Way, and the Coast to Coast route.

Monoculars were rare back then—they're hardly commonplace now, but this was pre-internet and I remember being delighted to find one in a second-hand camera shop. I think it cost me about £8.00. The reasons for buying a monocular were two-fold: firstly, they were recommended as a weight saving tip by *The Backpacker's Handbook*; more importantly, I have only one eye that focuses, so binoculars are of limited use.

After that summer, I used the monocular less frequently, and more recently it has gathered dust, surpassed by a newer model that offers better light capture and magnification. Jane considers the original to be useless—she says if reason had its way, I'd have sent it to the junk shop years ago. And she'd be right—if, that is, our possessions were all and only about utility. Instead, it has stayed in my desk, beside the pens and brushes and old sketchbooks that hold memories beyond any logical worth.

Recently, I had my eyes tested. I've used reading glasses for a decade, but two years ago I noticed my distance vision was weakening too. My optician gave me specs for driving and I found myself turning to them more and more. This time round, I asked if I could wear a contact lens instead—and it turns out I can.

Three weeks later and I'm still pinching myself when I look at the landscape! It's not just the extra clarity; by correcting a slight astigmatism the new lens widens my peripheral vision, and with only one functioning eye, that makes for a massive improvement. The other day, I compared it to the difference between an analogue TV, and a 50-inch widescreen with High Definition.

But if there's a downside to wearing the contact lens, it's that my reading glasses are now too strong. My optician suggested I buy some cheap readers. *You won't need expensive lenses, because the contact will already have corrected the shape of your eye. You might find your old glasses work well—if you still have them that is.*

And that's how I found myself sitting at the top of Pen-y-Fan, holding my old monocular to a newly lensed eye, watching the walkers on the ridge. The view, like memory, was blurred at first—but after a while, it came into focus. A group of young people were nearing the plateau, most of them wearing university hoodies.

As I was readying to go, they asked me to take their photo and to, my surprise, a girl passed me a camera rather than a phone. *You need to press the button quite hard,* she explained. After handing it back, she must have sensed my thoughts. *I know it looks a bit rubbish,* she apologised, *but I've had it for years and it takes good pictures.*

Sticks in each hand, I smiled as walked down the hill.

Words and pictures.

For the last three months I've been lecturing at the University of the West of England, teaching copy writing and professional practice. It's been as much a journey for me as my students, and a tonic, in the twilight of my career, to feel I have something to offer. But more than that, it's been a period of self-reflection, for if I've learned one thing about teaching undergraduates, it's that it requires looking as deeply into your own practice as theirs.

Often I start my lectures with a video, illustrating a notion that's caught the eye or snagged my memory. In part, I use these to settle the class, buying time for the inevitable stragglers. More substantially, I'm offering a sideways look at the creative processes, with a hint at its relevance to writers. Most times there's a tangential discussion, though occasionally I sense the gears and levers of my students' minds wondering if I've lost the plot.

Over the weeks, I've shown clips of Picasso at work, excerpts from documentaries, wildlife films, jazz improvisations, poetry readings... At my last lecture, we watched Damien Hirst discussing the paintings of Francis Bacon—one of my more esoteric selections. Yet despite a few blank looks, I was delighted when a student came up after class and said, *I'm beginning to see where you're coming from.*

In many ways, I learned to write through pictures. Not literally of course, but in the sense that for words to have depth of meaning, we're required to pay close attention. The same is true of painting. As Hirst points out, Bacon's works are much greater than our first impressions. Look closely at his images—so immediate and visceral—and you'll find they dissolve into thousands of marks: each a deliberate placement, whether delicate or violent, carefully considered, worked and reworked...

This is the craft behind the creation. And it comes less from technique than it does from care. More than any other advice I've given my students, is that they should pay attention to the detail. And by that I don't mean checking for typos; I mean being precise, taking heed of the words—shaping the sounds—to the point of exhaustion if necessary.

How long do you think it took to write that last paragraph? And how many edits would you guess I've made? If I told you in minutes, I'd be lying. And as for the changes—as I type this sentence I've gone back twice more. In the video of Bacon's paintings, Hirst draws attention to the image of an ear that's been overpainted so often the layers of pigment have congealed into sculpture.

I sense that all discovery is like this—a combination of creativity and craft. Creativity is what consciousness is to philosophy: something we experience and yet can't pin down. Craft, on the other hand, we can see and learn, and through long practice, even master. I was once rather sniffy about the idea of reworking, believing some 'deeper inspiration' to be the vital ingredient. But this is naïve; a misunderstanding of what craft is, and the role it plays.

In seeing craft as care rather than effort, we gain a different perspective. We also learn that process is not only necessary for the communication of our ideas, it's a gateway to creativity itself. In this respect, I suspect that most epiphanies—be they in art or science—come, as described by the mathematician Andrew Wiles, '*after stumbling round in the dark*'.

For me, the practice of refinement is as critical as ever—be that as a copy writer, essayist or blogger. First drafts are interminable: the movement from notion to form, at times glacial and always fractious. But to sense the shape emerging, to respond in turn—and to do so with truth—is the greatest joy in writing.

I hope my students feel that too, and come to see it all around them.

Blogging and how words have a life of their own

Early in my writing career, long before I was a 'published author', a friend and mentor advised me to share my work in whatever ways I could. The reason, she explained, *is that once you put your words out there, all manner of coincidence and possibility will emerge.* Shortly afterwards, I started *Views from the Bike Shed*, and the rest, as they say, is…

I retold that story last week to some students at the University of the West of England where I was giving a lecture on blogging. There's no better way, I suggested, to achieve a professional online presence and commit to the adventure that is the shaping and sharing of your thoughts. What follows, I said, may not be fame or fortune, but I guarantee it will surprise you.

By way of example, I described how from those humble beginnings, this blog became foundational to my degree, to my books, to articles being published elsewhere. Crafting the posts taught me the skills, and the care, I needed to be a serious writer—which I've since applied to both the corporate and personal sphere. To my amazement, writing is now what I do now for a living, and in ways I could never have imagined when starting out.

But perhaps the greatest joy of blogging is its 'message in a bottle' capacity for our posts to wash up on unexpected shores.

More than ten years ago I wrote a piece about (I thought) a long-forgotten outdoor writer named Derrick Booth. It touched a chord with hundreds of others in the backpacking community, and still today I receive kind comments and occasional emails in response. To my great delight, Derrick himself once wrote to me from California. I have dozens of other examples, from pieces I've written on bothies and wildflowers that somewhat inexplicably still have a high online ranking, to articles that were later published in journals, books and magazines. The most exciting—and frustrating—thing is that you can never tell what is going to resonate. Some of what I think of as my best pieces languish long-forgotten, others seem always to be making new connections.

I've made dozens of those through blogging—including a friendship with my all-time blogging hero, who ironically, turned out to live down the road. From similar tentative beginnings, Michelle at Vegplotting now writes for several magazines and newspapers, has a huge following and—being more sociable than me—international blog contacts that have taken her to the US, Canada and more.

Last week, after a long lay off, I wrote a short piece on, of all things, my collection of vacuum flasks. There were only a couple of comments on the blog, but I received dozens on a Facebook cross-post—that's a development I need to ponder. And I will. Because I've always approached my blogging as seriously as I do my other work. When I wrote that there's no better way 'to achieve a *professional* online presence…' the operative word in that sentence was aimed more at our attitude than any prospect of payment.

For when we publish—online or in print—we have a responsibility for our words that's fundamentally different from journaling or notebooks. It's not legal considerations that I'm hinting at here—it's that when we publish, in whatever form, we must care, and take responsibility for, the quality of what we say, as well as the tone of how we say it. Because, one way or the other, those words will find their way back to us, often in the most surprising of ways.

Yesterday morning I went to my favourite cafe—a little converted canal boat that I happened to write about last year. It's owner, Kelly, had been pleased with my quasi review, but little did I know she'd since followed more of my writing. As I ordered two eggs on toast, she rummaged in her bag, handing me a tiny plastic pouch: *I bought you this after reading your piece on introverts—it made me smile.*

You'll have to read the original post ('Red dots and the quiet life of an introvert') to understand the significance, but inside the bag she gave me was a red button badge. I think that's the oddest way that anyone has ever said thanks for something I've written—and you know what, it absolutely made my day.

No Time To Spare

Last week I happened to overhear the online funeral of a local resident—his hundredth birthday had been but a few months previous. I didn't know him, but the more I listened to the story of his life the more my admiration grew. He'd moved to our town when nearly ninety years old, had joined the bridge circle, the civic society, the conversational french group… eight clubs and societies in all; he played the piano every day, had driven until he was ninety-five, enjoyed companionship, exercised regularly … all this and he'd once had a pilot's licence, served in the war, danced… What a rich and full life!

The writer Ursula K. Le Guin died in 2018 aged 88—I've been reading a posthumously published collection of her blogs, *No Time to Spare*. They start from around 2010, which would have made her 80 years old when she began. By then she'd published dozens of books, won a string of international awards and was widely regarded as one of the greatest science fiction novelists of all time. She also penned essays, short stories, poems, the best book on how to write that I know (*Steering the Craft*) and of course—took up blogging.

This year I turn sixty, and still I often find myself saying, 'when I get old…' Which is ironic, because, of course, sixty is old—not in quite the way it used to be, but certainly the third stage of life, and a time when wisdom and reflection tends to takes precedence over physical prowess. All my working life I'd expected to be retired by this age—and after making prudent allowance there's no reason why I shouldn't be—but I find, now that it's possible, I approach the prospect with dread.

In the opening blog of Le Guin's collection she ponders a question in a residential survey—what do you like to do in your spare time? The tick boxes start with golf, and continue through shopping, TV, creative activities… 27 options in all. Le Guin reflects not so much on these, as the idea of having 'spare time', and what that means to those who're notionally retired. She concludes that she hasn't any; that all hers is taken because she is busy living.

And in Le Guin's case that was a full and rich endeavour too—creative, caring, campaigning to the end. I first discovered her work from a podcast interview—another communication form she embraced. And reading her blogs, there seems few limits to the scope of her enquiring mind. Last night, writing to a friend, I said that if—by some suspending of time and reality—I could host one of those imaginary dinner parties where you invite half a dozen people from history, Le Guin would be high on my guest list.

Because as I get older (note the change in emphasis there) the more determined I am to remain as curious as she was, to embrace change, not to be curmudgeonly—to be the very antithesis of the 'grumpy old man'. I've learned there are many virtues that come with age (Le Guin writes eloquently on this too) and that it's folly to chase rainbows by wishing ourselves younger—by looking backwards rather than ahead.

Nowadays, it's commonplace to see older folk cycling in lycra, running marathons, skiing down whatever... and in many ways this is truly excellent. I want to say fit; I want to travel; I have a very full bucket list of sorts. But I worry a little about the trend. Are we oldies, by filling our time with tick lists, by obsessing over fitness, by pursuing pleasure in whatever ways we can... finding truly positive purpose? Or are we staring into the pool of our lives only to see our reflection through eyes that ought to put on glasses?

For all I say 'we', I really mean 'me'. These worries are not meant as any criticism of others—rather, they are a deeper, more personal concern about how to find and maintain a purpose as I age. For some, playing golf or tennis may be the answer—and good for them—for others, it might be the daily practice of humility and grace—good for them too.

I'm not religious, and am not even sure that personal salvation gives any more meaning to life than the possibility of oblivion. But as I get older, I do feel keenly that we are part of one continuum—that the time we are gifted is but a moment at the end of a life-line that stretches back at least four billion years. And in that context, I'm conscious that the contribution we make is ultimately more satisfying, and meaningful, than any pleasure we take.

As for how to do that best, I'm still working and thinking it through.

This year I have a book to publish and should this pandemic ever end, perhaps—just perhaps—a PhD to begin. I'm yearning also to return to the mountains—to scale those heights that will only get harder with age, even if there's technology to help me. On the subject of which, one of my deepest determinations is never to sigh at its progress; to see it (and technology especially) as a map to explore, not a maze to be feared.

Most of all I'm determined to keep on learning.

For if I stopped, I'm sure I'd atrophy—and more quickly than from any lessening in my heart rate or weakening of my grip. I'm not sure I want—or have the spare time—to join eight clubs and societies; I'd hope that doing fewer things well might be just as rewarding. As Ursula K. Le Guin wrote in one of her very last blogs '…how rich we are in knowledge and in all that lies around us yet to learn. Billionaires all of us!'

Amen to that.

Commas—and signs of spring

Is there a surer sign of spring than the sight of a Comma on a country lane? Some would make a case for snowdrops or daffodils perhaps; my grandfather would have pointed to Ursa Major in the sky. There are lambs in the fields near my house, and the turning forward of the clocks is a milestone in the year. But for all these cues to the lengthening days, I'll stick with my first choice and the scalloped wings of one of our most remarkable butterflies.

Yesterday, as I walked the loop near my house, one was flying ahead of me. Each time I got near it would flit to a new clump of dandelions further down the verge. Or at least that's how it appeared, for it's just as probable I saw a number of specimens rather than one. The males are highly territorial, returning to the same bush or twig where they bask in the sun and wait for a mate to pass by. I suppose it might have been a single female, but if so, she wasn't stopping to lay eggs on the nettles and currants that are now the most common plants on which to find its larvae.

I say 'now' because in the past it was the Hop that was the Comma's favoured foodplant. By the early years of last century, with the decline of Hop farming, the butterfly was confined to but a handful of counties—including as it happens, Monmouthshire where I live. Even as recently as the Seventies its distribution was confined to the South and West, which explains why it wasn't until I moved from my native Northumberland that I first recorded a sighting in my little Observer's Book of Butterflies.

Happily today, the Comma is one of our most successful species. Having made a spectacular comeback, it can be found across all but the most northern counties of Great Britain, and it's thought this is due to the changing of its larval foodplant to the Common Nettle. Milder winters will have helped too, for it's a species that hibernates as an adult—those I saw yesterday will have spent the winter camouflaged in the bushes and barns along my route.

But here I am getting all nerdy when you can read this in books or on websites. You can learn, too, about its fascinating ability to produce offspring variants; one of which has an annual lifecycle, the other producing a second brood in summer. It's these which are so vibrant in the spring. My trusty Observer's book describes their colour as tawny or fulvous: I had to look it up—what a fabulous new word to have learned.

And that's appropriate, for I think it's the surprise of seeing the Comma that I like the most. When I first moved south, I'd assume that glimpse of russet brown to be a Tortoiseshell or perhaps a Fritillary (*though surely too early I'd say*). Three decades later, there's still a delight in that first spring sighting—the signal that summer's on its way—and somehow more so than in spotting the obvious Orange Tip or pale yellow Brimstone, neither of which—come to think—have I seen this year.

On Saturday, I'm travelling to Pembrokeshire. That in itself is a sign of spring; of rebirth and renewal of a different sort. There should be Small Coppers on the Coast Path and I expect there'll be Peacocks, which overwinter, like the Comma, in the lanes by our cottage. Butterflies have fascinated me for fifty years; the joy of seeing them never fades. Our neighbours have two boys who also take an interest; the youngest is the age I was when I first recorded what I'd seen. I hope he too will witness springs and seasons as abundant as mine have been.

Haston Vallot rucksack

Unless you're a mountaineer—and even then, you'd have to be one of a certain age—I very much doubt you could name, let alone recognise the significance of, the rucksack in the picture above. For most folk it would be something that's stored in the loft, deprived of light until tipped or car-booted for few quid at best. And yet, in its time, the Haston Vallot was quite the thing, as was the climber, after whom it's named.

I bought mine in June 1980, at the start of the long summer break from university. My parents had recently separated: my mother moving to a tiny flat; my father not really an option to stay with. With nowhere to else go, I decided to walk from Coast to Coast. And so began a path that, in a sense, I'm following still.

The man in the shop said it was definitely the one to buy. I remember being sceptical: it was expensive, and most rucksacks in those days had metal frames and multiple pockets. This was different, he explained, an *alpiniste style* which didn't use a structured chassis—the hip belt and straps would do the work, he said, and what's more, if I progressed from walking to climbing, I'd already have the right equipment…

Ten minutes later I owned my first piece of mountaineering gear. I bought a sleeping mat too—and a Trangia stove that's still going strong. Somewhere along the way, I acquired a tent and sleeping bag; they weighed a tonne, but they saw me from Whitehaven to Robin Hood's Bay and afterwards most of the Pennine Way.

In the late Seventies, Karrimor was the UK's leading rucksack brand. They were known for good quality and innovative designs. The model I bought was named after Dougal Haston, the first Britain to succeed on the direct route of the Eiger's north face. His bold approach was an inspiration for a generation of mountaineers, pioneering what are now known as alpine style ascents in the Himalaya and beyond. My memory tells me that he designed the outer loop, which stows the belt and stops it from snagging if you haul the pack up a cliff—but I can't be sure and suspect I'm getting a bit geeky… What's more relevant is that by the early Eighties all packs looked a little like this, and the ones we use today owe their heritage to these early designs.

Returning to my purchase, after that first summer it transitioned with me from walking to climbing, just as the salesman said. I took it to the Alps, on hut tours in Austria, and for years it carried my rock gear round the crags of Northumberland. It's a regular presence in my photo albums of those years—like a hidden clue, of the sort a TV detective would spot.

And if they ever came looking, they'd not take long to find it—for I never got round to storing my sack in the loft. In fact, I used it this week to go camping with my eldest son, retracing a walk over the Preseli Hills that we'd first made eleven years ago. He was a teenager then, and the story of that trip became the title piece of my book *Counting Steps*. It seemed appropriate for our return, though my nostalgic mumblings cut little ice as I fumbled with stiff zips and broken buckles—but that's another story, for another book maybe.

Sadly, Karrimor are no longer in business—they went bust in 2003, though the trademark limps on after purchase by Sports Direct. Dougal Haston is gone too; he died skiing in Leysin, not far, as it happens, from my house in France. But I reckon my old sack has a few years in it yet—there's evidently a repair shop in Lancashire that can sort those zips, and despite the odd creaky joint, I can still smile as I shoulder the weight—and the memories—it holds.

Interlude:
Second Steps

So you've taken the plunge, signed up for your blog and are raring to go... Suddenly, that screen looks ominously blank. Which I'd suggest is no bad thing, because—not withstanding some of my previous advice—in many ways, I wish I'd paused a moment or two before publishing my first post.

Certainly, I'd like to have known then a little of what I do now.

Such is the way with journeys of discovery, but it's not my intention to map out a route, because prescription in these matters isn't helpful. Instead, what I might usefully offer, is some thoughts on those early roads I travelled; reflections on my going astray rather than advice on which way to go.

And those missteps began right at the start.

For *Views from the Bike Shed* is quite possibly the worst blog title I could have come up with.

Or at least, that's what a blogging consultant would advise. Is it about bikes, they'd say... or sheds... or a webcam overlooking my garden? And, even more to the point, what's its purpose and vision, it's theme and target audience; what are the unique selling points that will make it search engine friendly...

Can you tell I don't think much of consultants?

In fairness, they'd have a point.

Blogs work best when they have a clear theme, and reflecting that focus in your title (which is likely also to be your blog's web address) is a good idea. I'm sceptical of bloggers worrying too much about search engine optimisation and it's like—therein lies distraction, pseudo science, and at worst, compromise to the quality of our work—but if we can incorporate good practice into something as basic as the name of our blog, then that would seem consistent with the professionalism I spoke of earlier.

Occasionally, I envy my blogging friends who have a more defined focus for their writing than mine—not least because it's helpful in building an audience. Any cursory look at the 'blogosphere' will confirm that subjects such as travel, cookery, gardening, fashion, sports… all lend themselves well to the format. Clarity of your subject also confers expertise, and even without that claim, it will gather like minded readers. It's no coincidence that successfully themed blogs, often morph into broader websites with more sophisticated structures and content.

In part, this is because the targeting of their subject matter, together with a regular readership, can lead to endorsement, sponsorship and advertising opportunities. It can also, from the perspective of those us wanting to be professional writers, add credibility and show a track record, when, for example, pitching ideas and articles to more mainstream magazines or websites.

For many of the young and aspiring writers I've taught, a well themed and well curated blog can be a fabulous statement—and statement of intent—when they're looking for their first opportunities, not just as traditionally published authors, but in careers such as journalism, PR, or marketing communications.

For all that, if my first reflection is to avoid vague titles (or ploughing a furrow of the mixed reflections from middle age) the second returns me to my home ground of blogging for writers—with emphasis again on that last word.

And it's simply to be aware, or perhaps to 'beware' of what you wish for.

In reading the paragraphs above is there anything of relevance to your writing ambitions? Do you want to pursue advertising and sponsorship, or use a blog as a route to a career? Are you struggling to find a specialist subject and, like me, wanting the freedom to write as you please?

These questions matter.

I know of a number of bloggers who've develop careers in fashion and travel journalism. I know of others who've themed their blogs on less overtly commercial lines, and yet still built considerable followings. Mum-blogging, for example, is a huge niche, so too activities such as adventure pursuits, camping, fanzines… And if that's what you're working towards, then go for it.

But don't forget that it's the writing which counts.

If as writers we become more concerned with the commercial payback or the prospect of some freebies, then in my experience something is lost along the way. *Views from the Bike Shed* has no endorsements, no advertising, no possible prospect of becoming commercially successful... because that's not its purpose.

And this, I think, is where the consultants miss the critical question. Why is it that we write?

Or putting this slightly differently, what is it we are hoping to achieve? As a blogger, I'm constantly asking myself if my posts and the words they contain reflect that ambition; probing my motivations and striving to ensure they don't stray from what matters most.

It took me many years to be fully confident in *what I do*—and to be equally happy with *what I don't*. I'm not a poet, nor do I write fiction, though elements of those genres influence my style. What's more, I don't write a diary or keep a journal or even (dare I admit this) take many notes. My writing space is personal essays, in long form, and blogs. I want to write from the tradition of Montaigne and Orwell, pondering on life and the lessons it teaches us. I write for myself, though always conscious it's not about me.

And if that's all a bit muddled, well that's why *Views from the Bike Shed* is too. Because it reflects my interests and ambitions, and my imperfect attempts to stay as true to those as I can.

Which is just the sort of juxtaposition that brings me fresh to my keyboard every day.

When a journey becomes an itinerary, we lose something of that sense of exploration and the joy of discovery which comes with it. Similarly, overthinking can lead to indecision, crippling our confidence with a focus on risks rather than rewards.

Yesterday I published a post about visiting an old flooded quarry near my house in West Wales. As I had sat on the cliffs there were young people below me, jumping from the rocks, shrieking with delight at the moments of falling between land and sea. Some of their party were too nervous to commit, their anxiety worsening the longer they held back. And yet, when they eventually leapt, their glee was the greatest of all— the sounds of their joy spilling into the wind...

So pause if you will—but not for too long.

Blue and grey and all the colours in between

Last week I visited Newcastle and the North-east of England. It's where I grew up, where I lived until my late twenties and where my son is now a few weeks from completing his architecture qualifications. His presence there for eight years has been simultaneously a wrench and a magnet, a tear to the heart and a stitch that binds the soul. The sense of love and loss has lingered since the evening I left him at his halls with two suitcases, a wedge of cash and strict instructions to spend it all on partying not books.

In truth, the rent is more than the miles between us.

For all it is distant, Newcastle is no more than a day's journey by car, and this dreadful pandemic aside, driving north has become a regular family trip, uniting us in more ways than one. A love of the region has crossed the generations and even filtered its way into Jane, who looks forward to our visits as much as me. But neither she nor my son can share the depth of belonging that comes from what I guess we call roots—a word that hints at the gravity of the ground from which we grow.

The picture above is of Tynemouth Longsands; my childhood home was a mile beyond the prominent spire on the horizon. When we visited one evening last week, Jane laughed at the 'proper hard' Geordies, taking a dip in the slate grey waters, a chill wind blowing in from Norway. I told her this was where we'd learned to swim, in costumes my mum ran up on her sewing machine. Cold came with the territory—and now I come to think, I've no fixed memory of the ocean here ever being blue.

But I have other recollections: of crabbing in the rocks, of picnics on the sands, of lifeboats and bonfires... of times with my brothers and friends, always by the sea. And later, of days walking this coast, escaping from a father with manic depression, which we didn't understand, and a temper I thought that all dads had. It's strange that for a place I miss so much, the resounding echo could so easily have been one of fear.

That it isn't, is in large part a choice I made. For our memories—good and bad—are always a fiction of sorts. My narrative is that this is the place I came through; and that further north especially, in the hills and moors of Northumberland, where I found my strength, became fiercely independent, and understood that moving on requires letting go too...

It's astonishing that I should write those words so fluidly and without prior thought; that thirty years since I left the North East something so obvious seems like a revelation. The irony is that in my pursuing a new and better future, I moved so far from the place that draws me back.

Only recently I read that to transplant a shrub is traumatic to its growth, the more so the longer it's established—evidently, a fair proportion will not survive. To do much the same to ourselves is similarly stressful, with an equal need for care and attention to timing.

Could I move back to the place I left in order to get to where I am now? Would returning to the land of my youth be a coming full circle or a wretched retreat? Is the pull I feel an irresistible truth, or a nostalgic lament that, like Houseman's blue remembered hills, cannot come again?

Only this week I was talking to a friend who said he felt something of the same about Devon; that he was never more at home than when the soil was iron-red; when walking the land where generations of his ancestors had lived without question. He too felt the counterweight of a yearning to belong and the pull of a new life found and now founded elsewhere.

In a few weeks, my son will complete his training; in a handful more the lease on his flat expires. I might come home for a while, he said; he was referring to Wales. There's a part of me delighted at the prospect, and another that's willing him to remain, to find a job up north—to plant his mark in the earth which I dug up.

The truth is, I shall pine if he stays and ache if he leaves.

Last week as we sat in the dunes watching the light fade, I was thinking of all these things. And it occurred to me, in the way that coincidence takes us unawares, that my son is almost the age I was when I left for Wales. I thought of the turns I've taken, of the skies and seas—blue and grey and every colour in-between—that have passed over my head and under my feet with the turning of the years.

And I smiled.

There's time I reasoned, for these matters to resolve; for the roots I've laid down—and those my son will in turn—to grown deeper or be replanted as we wish.

It was twilight when we reached the car and took the road along the cliffs, passing the streets I still know by name. Turning west, I couldn't have said if I was heading for home or leaving it behind. After all these years, the sense of love and loss is as real and charged ever.

And long may it continue—for there are few things that make me feel more alive.

Welsh bothies

Of all the blogs I have written, many of them crafted and personally revealing, it is this inconspicuous piece—a largely straight informative article—that continues to attract the largest number of visitors to Views from the Bike Shed. The reason is almost certainly its simple and well defined title, which is perfect for search engine optimization. I include it here more for its 'pulling power' than any particular merit—for all that I've rather come to like it

There are eight mountain bothies in Wales. All but one is maintained by the Mountain Bothies Association, which has care of over a hundred across the UK, the majority in Scotland. They are simple shelters, located in wild places, most usually at a far distance from other accommodation—typically, they're old farm buildings, shepherd's huts, occasionally purpose built emergency shelters like the one on the Cheviot.

My favourite in Wales is Nant Rhys, about an eight mile walk from Devil's Bridge but accessible by a shorter route if you prefer—it's possible to cycle there too. The old farmhouse has two rooms, each with a wood burning stove; there are some basic sleeping platforms, a few pots and pans, a room upstairs for more to sleep if needed. Then it gets a bit posh—there's a wood store at the back, a tank for washing water (drinking water from the stream) and a long drop earth toilet with perhaps the finest view of any loo I know.

I first went there with Daniel and remember us looking at stars in the blackest sky—the area around Nant Rhys has some of the lowest light pollution south of the Highlands. I keep suggesting we return, take his younger brother perhaps, but he's not been so keen since girlfriends came on the scene. I reckon he'll be up for a trip next year though, especially now he wants to learn to drive—that feels like an excellent bargaining chip!

Jane can't see the attraction—they're dirty and smelly she says, and I'm not sitting on one of those outdoor loos! More than that, she's worried an axe-man will murder us in our sleeping bags. In reality, there's a greater chance of being assaulted in the city and exactly the same toilets have been installed at Skomer Island, by the Wildlife Trust—but somehow they're more acceptable. I'm not suggesting we should disregard safety, and if you're a nervous type I'd not recommend going alone, but there are reasons why volunteers maintain these shelters.

And chief among them is that they're fabulous places to escape to—to get away from all the stuff we accumulate, to seek freedom in the very opposite of what ties us down; to connect with things that are simpler and more profound. For me, if half the fun is the getting to them, the other half is simply being there.

Bothies are free to use—you don't have to be a member of the MBA—all that's asked is that you follow the bothy code and leave it much the same as you found it. You'll need a sleeping bag, a thermal mat, a stove and basic food—don't rely on pans being there—and some sort of lighting too; LEDs are best and head torches are useful. Personally, I like to take some scotch, but I guess that's optional.

For years the precise locations of shelters were not generally publicised, but the policy changed a few years ago and grid references are available on various websites and even some books. In Wales, there's one bothy in the Brecon Beacons, four in the Elenydd and three in Snowdonia. For those in the North of England, there are ten in the Pennines and Lake District.

If the idea of a bothy is appealing but a bit too basic, you could try the 'five star' version at Claerddu near the Teifi Pools—it has a flush loo, gaslighting and even a stove. A step up again is Black Sail Hostel in the Ennerdale Valley, where they serve meals and good beer—it's the nearest thing to an alpine hut in the UK, but obviously, it's not free. There are plenty of bunkhouses too.

But there's something special about the real thing.

When I was last at Nant Rhys I read a comment in the logbook from a chap who went there regularly—he'd written, *I love this place*.

And I thought, that's surely reason enough.

Kelly and Victor

This is the only review of a film I've written. Shortly after posting it, I met Niall Griffiths at a lecture and learned that he'd read the piece. 'Thanks for the blog,' he growled at me over a beer. 'You got it; you totally f***ing nailed it...' Praise indeed!

The novels of Niall Griffiths are among the most raw and savage of contemporary narratives. His better known titles include *Sheepshagger, Runt* and *Wreckage.* In reading his books, you're made intimate with an underworld of drugs, sex and violence...

And never more so than his 2002 novel, *Kelly and Victor*—mention of which induces a sharp whistle from those who had the stomach to finish it. The story is so intensely disturbing that, of all Griffiths' books, it's the one I'd have thought least likely to be made into a film.

Which just goes to show how much I know.

This week *Kelly and Victor* opened at independent cinemas across the UK. Its portrayal of the protagonists' destructive love affair is as eye-wateringly graphic, as deeply perturbing—and as tender and empathetic—as is the book.

Kelly and Victor is the story of two young people, swimming in a whirlpool of abuse. The psychological damage they've suffered takes its physical form in their lovemaking—the intensity of which momentarily releases them from the vicious spiral. But in so doing, stirs an equally addictive, and ultimately tragic, compulsion.

Directed by Kieran Evans, the film stars Antonia Campbell Hughes and Julian Morris. It is beautifully photographed and carefully paced to maintain the tension; it does the book justice without being a slavish copy. And at ninety minutes, it's thankfully not too long—something that's the curse of so many mainstream movies.

Campbell Hughes is an especially inspired casting; her portrayal of the frail and elfin Kelly is both believable and entirely absent of sentimentality—for me, she was the standout of the film. The soundtrack would be my second choice: wonderfully evocative of the mixed up, fucked up, under-world inhabited by the characters. A close third: the cinematic treatment of the urban landscapes, reminiscent of the original *Get Carter*.

Actually, that film isn't an unfair comparison on the whole. Because, as with *Get Carter*, behind the superficial brutality lies a deeper compassion. The genius of *Kelly and Victor* is not that it's unflinchingly profane—but that despite this, you care about the characters. And the reason is that in being so flawed, they are also deeply human.

The British Film Institute has chosen *Kelly and Victor* as their pick of the week. There are plenty of detailed reviews online and frankly, there's not much I can add here.

Except, as I came out of the arts centre, I was struck by how intense the experience had been—how much I'd enjoyed it; how engaged with the film I'd been. In recent years I've come to loathe contemporary cinema—the predictability of yet another Spielberg-inspired white-knuckle opening scene, literally sends me to sleep.

This was different—it was cinema as it should be; real drama—and it takes its cue from an almost lost heritage of great British movies. We need more films like *Kelly and Victor*. But for that to happen I guess we need more people to make the effort.

Go see for yourself.

Lists for blogging—and for life

Most bloggers I know keep lists, at least in their head if not on their PC or jotter. I use all three, as well as my phone and the blackboard in our kitchen and the back of a packet or two. When stressed, list-making is my go-to relief, as if ticking all the items will eliminate the source of the angst. Get everything done, I say to myself, and there'll be time to relax... and start a new list tomorrow.

For *Views from the Bike Shed*, I make a note of the posts I might write, a store of ideas for when inspiration or memory fails me. It's part of the curation process I say, the planning for a varied output that will keep my readers engaged. There are currently eleven items in my notebook, dozens more on my phone and many more that have been consigned to the bin.

On the page beside me as I type is a list that includes: The Three Peaks of Abergavenny; Collecting Jugs; Digital Minimalism; Girls Own Paper and Bookmarks. How many of these, I wonder, will make it into print? Two would be good going; three a marvel. And those I've mentioned are the most likely; there's another six I might as well cross off now.

Perhaps the problem is not so much with the making of my lists as with the nature of our epiphanies. What seems so vital and vibrant in the moment, tends to fade as the passage of time dulls our enthusiasm. How often have I woken from slumber, written down some putatively genius insight only to read it a week later and think, 'In your dreams, Mark; literally, in your dreams...'

But is this such a bad thing? Because for all that some ideas are lost—and this blog is sparser as a result—isn't the unconscious mind also acting as a sort of quality control? And frankly, if it were not for a little temporal distance between my thoughts and my keyboard, the blog you're reading might all too easily be called *'Rants'* rather than *'Views'* from the Bike Shed.

And that wouldn't do.

Because sounding off seldom works out well and almost never if done too often. Indeed, rants by their nature have an impact only if they break the pattern of the norm; to be permanently raging is invariably to become blinkered and somewhat deaf to others. The exceptions that prove this rule are those rare talents such as Jeremy Clarkson, whose columns, far from being true rants, are actually humorous vexations on the absurdities we encounter.

Which makes me wonder if my list-making—and my failure to follow through—is any different to everyday life? We all have our passing fancies; intentions that sound great in the pub or as presented on TV. But when it comes to taking action, they suddenly don't seem so compelling. For years I've been saying to Jane that we really must go to Hampton Court, after all, it's not that far... so long as we set off early, and avoid the London traffic and book in advance...

In her turn, Jane says I should be less driven; try to enjoy what's around me instead of always looking ahead. It's fine to be doing, she says, so long as you don't forget about being. Actually, those words are mine not hers—she'd put it more plainly and tell me to stop obsessing over things that can wait. And why, she'd ask, am I so focused on striving that I lose sight of what we already have?

She's right, of course, and yet I can't shake the habit.

There's a body of research that claims achievement is fundamental to our happiness and sense of self-worth. I feel it keenly, together with a sense of responsibility to others as well as myself. I'm sure this explains my reluctance to retire and certainly my intention never to stop writing.

I'm conscious, too, of not wasting the opportunity and privilege we've been afforded. Imagine a life in which your ambitions were thwarted, your chances proscribed by custom or lack of resources. Such was the lot of most people (women especially) for millennia—and in truth, it remains the case in large parts of the world. My parents in law, two former school teachers, have visited over one hundred countries in their retirement—an achievement that's unthinkable in historical terms.

Theirs, of course, is a different kind of list to what we began with. Like those I keep of books I've read, it looks backwards not forward, recording rather than prompting. There's a danger, with lists of this type, that their length becomes more important than their purpose—but at their best, they can be a trove of memory, imbuing a sense of a life well-lived. The concept of a 'bucket list' has become commonplace parlance, and a reflection of a predominantly secular outlook on the ticking of our clocks: *carpe diem*; you only live once; eternity is an awfully long time…

Which inclines me to think I've been rambling on quite enough. What started as a notion about blogging has morphed, through a series of unplanned diversions, into reflections on the good life.

And maybe that's a fitting conclusion: that as writers the purpose of our lists is not so much to schedule our output as to remind us of the wealth of the choices we have on offer. This is a good and wonderful thing, so long as we know also when to stop.

Stick

I grew up in the North East of England at a time when family holidays seldom amounted to more than one week a year. We spent ours at towns and resorts which today would seem little further away than a day trip destination. One year we travelled to Whitby, another to Edinburgh, and once, to Berwick on Tweed. There was a trip to Keswick too, which my father, in one of his bouts of depression, refused at the last minute to go on—my Mum took me and my brothers regardless, travelling by bus and train, then walking up hills every day to tire us out.

In some ways it's not surprising that my father didn't come, because mostly he hated holidays—it was only later, in the Seventies when he could lie on a beach in the Spanish sun, that he was ever happy to leave home. Whether that was because of his depression or his inherent demeanour I don't know, but I do remember the rows just to get him to go for a picnic. When my mother learned to drive, she at last found the freedom that would convince her to leave for good.

But the exception to this rather gloomy beginning for a blog post were our visits to Hawes in the Yorkshire Dales. My father had been an evacuee there—arriving as a family unit with his brother and my grandmother; presumably, my grandfather was enlisted at the time. They lodged in a manor on the edge of the town and at some point moved to a farm across the fields from what later became the Wensleydale Creamery.

On our first visit my father took us to the 'large house', and I remember we were all peering over the wall into a bramble filled garden when a voice shrieked. 'Are you looking at my wilderness!' Leaning out of the upstairs window was what I took to be a witch with long ragged hair, tattered clothes and boney arms—very much the 'lady in the attic' look. Which turned out to be not so far off the mark...

After explanations and introductions, we were invited in for tea. The present owner was, to use a phrase of the time, completely barking! The house was a ramshackle ruin of peeling paper, broken china, and musty chairs. She claimed to keep her husband upstairs in a cupboard, which I was later told not to take too literally, but never quite shook the suspicion of its truth. Whenever we passed by, my father would tell stories of the times he'd spent there and in the area.

Looking back, there were few places that my father enthused over as much as the Yorkshire Dales. I sometimes wonder if the reason for this was that his own father was away for the time he was there? My grandfather was a uniquely wonderful man, but I'm under no illusion that he wasn't always the best or most present of dads. There was a bond between my father and his mother that I sense came from those years and was associated in his mind to the places they'd stayed.

He took us often to the nearby village of Gayle and a brook he called Belia Banks, which I can't find on the map and may be spelling incorrectly, but it's where we went looking for—and caught—crayfish. We also went to Aysgarth Falls and the Buttertubs Pass and the cheese factory; in the town we visited a ropemaker and, nearby, a chap who made clogs, from whom my mother bought a miniature pair which sat for years on our hearth at home...

And somewhere in all of this, I acquired a walking stick, of the size suitable for an eight-year-old boy.

That stick is the second oldest object I have from my childhood. Beating it by a few years is a French faience bowl, but as that has sat in the china cupboard and storage boxes for much of the last fifty years, it doesn't carry the same store of memories. In truth, because it's so small, I've not been able to use the stick for most of those years either—but always I treasured it, and my sons have played with it and somehow it's never not been 'around'. Currently it lives in an umbrella stand by the coat rack.

Before writing this post I took the time to look at it again, examining the knots and burrs, the careful bending of the wood to shape the handle. It's probably made from hazel or ash and has a brass ferrule that rattles because the shaft has shrunk—there's a tiny split near the base of the cane which I hope can be repaired. At one time it was varnished, but only remnants remain, the years of wear and rough play removing all but a few flecks here and there.

But you know, there's only so much you can say about a stick—or indeed, that needs to be said. Because it's not so much the thing in and of itself that's important. It's the connection it holds to those holidays: to the times we stayed at the farm B&B and drank goat's milk, and chased the geese over the field each morning, me waving my stick to drive them… and to the names and places that are with me still, and the memory of my father for once not hating it quite so much.

It has just occurred to me now that when our first son was born, Jane and I took him with us to Hawes for a holiday that summer. We carried him in a backpack on our walks: to Gayle and the Buttertubs Pass, to Aysgarth Falls and the ropemaker in town… I'm sure we must have been to a stick maker too… and certainly, we bought some cheese from the creamery, and looked for the large house and saw the fields of geese…

Oh, how life—and our lives—turn in circles.

Bleaklow

Bleaklow is not a good place to walk alone. It's one of the darkest sections of the Pennine Way, a huge seething bog, a misty featureless plateau, a place for lost souls. Or so the reputation goes.

Saturday it was cold, the sun struggling to break through. I parked on the Snake Road and set off into the wind—alone, save for my trusty dog Peeps who was eyeing the sheep and pulling at the lead. Best to get it over with I thought, pushing on up the hill. The path was mostly slabs—so much for a seething bog—in less than an hour I reached the Wainstones and Bleaklow Head.

On first impressions there's little here, even the peat has been eroded—a sad wooden pole leaning out of the summit cairn. It feels lonely, not a place to linger, though by the numbers of walkers I'd passed it must be popular enough. I took off my hat and coat and set off towards Torside Resevoir; if I kept my head down, I might get there in an hour.

Just over the rise I noticed a white stone in the peat hags; it seemed out of place amongst the gritstones. I looked again; perhaps it was a bag left by the slab layers? Some urge made me walk over to investigate, plodging through the sticky peat towards the heather. When I was a few feet from the stone, it moved—bounding up the hag and stopping to look at me before curling up again. A mountain hare!

I stood and waited. Another appeared—this one had lost its winter coat—then another behind it, and another, a white one this time. I had never seen hares on the moors before. They seemed untroubled by my presence, scampering about the peat, rising on their hind legs for a better view. A group of walkers I'd overtaken well below the summit passed me, perhaps wondering what I was doing, standing ankle deep in the mire. 'There ain't nowt much up 'ere,' one of them joked.

A little further on, the path follows a stream, the water dribbling over slabs into a series of pools, fresh with weed and moss. Sitting here I saw many things: a dipper, a golden plover, two grouse, some wagtails, a kestrel hovering in the valley below. Peeps sat with me, drinking the water from the pool and sniffing at my hot cross buns but not partaking.

From Clough Edge I mentally traced the line over Black Hill, the next section of the Way. The wind was whipping up white horses on the reservoir; I noticed the other walkers making their way on the lower path. Coming down the ridge I met the Park Ranger. He asked about my walk and we talked about the slabs that had improved access, encouraging many more people to visit. 'It's a funny thing,' he said, 'folk tend to do this walk in groups, but it's always the lone walkers who see the most.'

He confirmed it was a dipper and a golden plover I'd seen. I told him about the hares. Did they still have their winter coats, he asked? Magnificent, we both agreed, and he left me to see for himself.

An hour behind my schedule, I walked past the reservoir to meet my lift at Crowden.

Hairdressing and chairs

When my son Michael was small, we asked him (as you do) what he'd like to be when he grew up? 'A hairdresser and a chair,' he replied. We used to tease him about this, and it wasn't long before he'd changed chair to 'Chairman', realising this better fitted our middle class expectations; no further mention was made of hairdressing.

All this seems so recent that it came as a shock when he returned home from school with a list of subject choices for next year's timetable. The literature and advice from the school was interesting.

What struck me most was the emphasis on career planning. There was extensive detail on how certain subjects would open up opportunities in the job market. There was data too—indeed there's always been data from the school (most of it incomprehensible, but impressive to some no doubt)—detailing how many A-stars were achieved last year; what were the percentage pass rates, etc., etc.

There's fierce competition for the best pupils. At the open evening, one teacher went so far as to say that their subject was 'gold standard' as far as universities were concerned. True perhaps, but how about telling Michael why it's interesting to learn about history, or geography, or drama...

I'm not generally critical of developments in education, rather the reverse. My boys' school is a shining example of how standards have improved. It's just disappointing that the school doesn't seem to have the confidence to promote learning for its own sake. Even for thirteen year-olds, they seems to believe that what matters most to their parents (for I'm sure it's largely targeted at them) is the extent to which their children's subject choices fit into a wider career path.

Universities are almost as bad; a recent prospectus that passed my desk was full of the jargon and pseudo babble of business. It gave more prominence to the KPIs on post graduate employment than it did to the subjects it had to offer. The implication was crass; studying here is a means to an end; after all, what else would you want? Well, what about the difference that knowledge can make to your life; what about learning because it enriches you in more ways than money?

Perhaps I shouldn't be surprised. I recall one of the mums at the boys' junior school priming her son with past papers in preparation for the year-six SATs. Only a few years older than this unfortunate child, one of the graduate trainees at work told me he'd chosen his degree course (business studies with accounting or something equally dull) because, from an early age he'd known he was going to be *passionate about logistics*.

Oh, get a life!

I can't think it's coincidental that so many people drop any semblance of interest in academic study once their qualifications are in the bag. Amongst my work colleagues there's a host of degrees and professional qualifications but the main topic of conversation on Mondays is last weekend's football. I'm branded an 'intellectual' because I read a few books and write a bit. The irony is that the business community then spends a fortune trying to convincing their staff of the benefits of 'lifetime learning'.

I hope I'm not snobby. We all need down time, there's nothing wrong with football and it would be an odd world if we sat around discussing Schopenhauer, fascinating though he is. Underneath the banter people have all sorts of interests: my PA loves Shakespeare; a close colleague collects Moorcroft pottery; another became animated today as he told me of the year he spent studying locusts; my boss speaks excellent French; my previous boss painted watercolours. But it is sad that these interests are often hidden or repressed—something to be dreamed about, but not acted on; like my own secret wish to have been a baker.

There's hope though.

Yesterday I walked with Michael along the cycle path at Calne. It was evening and the bats were coming out, moths too. The dog scampered after a squirrel and I almost thought we'd lost her. Michael talked of his interest in drama, and painting; how he liked history and the way it explained the present; the new subjects he'd like to try; sports too. Never once did he say this or that would be good for getting a job; we didn't discuss pass rates; it didn't matter what other people thought was cool.

And we neither of us mentioned hairdressers or chairs.

Puzzle

You should bring an object with a strong emotional connection, said the preparatory notes to a writing class I attended last week. If you can't have it to hand, then one you can hold in your mind's eye; something you can feel, in every sense of the word. Had it not been an online class, I might have prepared more fully—instead, I reached instinctively to the drawers of my desk where the puzzle resides.

As it has for more than forty years.

I'm not exactly sure when I acquired it, but it must have been around my early teens—and it was a Christmas present, I know that. Or at least I do in the sense that it's my fixed, if often fallible, memory, rather than in any evidential proof: the puzzle isn't the sort of item you'd be holding in a photograph, and as it's spent most of the last four decades in the dark, it hasn't even faded with age.

Describe your object, the tutor said: *square, smart, controlled—circles and hoops—patterns and archways—click, rattle roll...* And then the emotions it holds, she continued...

Anyone who's attended a writing workshop will recognise these sorts of exercises. I'm not very good at them—the speed at which we're expected to respond is too quick for my liking. Often, to be honest, they're a bit 'touchy feely'—and there's always, lurking in my mind, the fear of what I call the curse of the workshop genre: snippets that are seldom as deep as we believe at the time.

Yet, when I look back at my notes, I'm struck by the visceral tone of what's on the page: *I love it, actually, I love it a lot—a little square box of my childhood—controlled, calm—better and different to others—the 'winning position', it says on the back...*

Apt!

I don't know what forces drove me to write that, and to underline it too.

The puzzle was merely a stocking present—I doubt anyone else in my family would remember it, or knew how much I liked it at the time. It's a solid little item, and as a young boy it felt like I owned something rather sophisticated. I was good at solving it too—skilled at the deft nudges and delicate balance it requires. At that age, I used to nurture the idea of everything being controlled and ordered, of having a desk, and an office… and handwriting that was neater than my father's…

How odd is that?

The person I feared most in the world, controlled through a plastic puzzle?

Is that what psychologists—psychiatrists even—might say of my holding onto it? For all they might, I wasn't conscious of that then, nor have I been all these years. The puzzle is just a present that felt smart (a word I used repeatedly in my notes) and which by some random happenstance I never threw out…

And so it's stayed with me through college and jobs and houses and children… all the hoops and circles of my life and the lives that have mattered to me. Is it possible that sometimes the objects we hold onto have meaning simply because we've done just that? That their significance grows in direct proportion to their age—as if by discarding them we would be forsaking our past?

The artist Michael Landy has long fascinated me—in a performance piece titled 'Break Down' he famously destroyed every object he owned, including his passport and keys. The shredding of a painting by Gary Hume, a fellow Young British Artist, was a talking point at the time. But it was the destruction of his childhood toys, and his father's sheepskin coat, that brought me close to tears. It has always struck me as unspeakably brave.

I sometimes wonder what will happen to the objects around me when I'm dead. Any significance attached to the puzzle rests with me, not those who will sort through my drawers. Most likely, they'll find some items of sentimental value—but who wants a collection of moths, or the detritus of a life that's run its course? I wouldn't want that from my forefathers.

That said, there are a few small heirlooms I keep; my grandfather's prayer book; a golden cravat pin; a clip that's shaped like a fish. Will the next generation—or the one which follows—care, or even know of their heritage? Entropy must always increase with time.

We know that objects can only ever be a proxy for a past that must eventually be lost. We know too, that real life isn't like my puzzle—that it's not controlled, or always smart, or never fading with age… and that any so-called winning position—no matter how deftly nudged or delicately balanced—cannot be held indefinitely. The square box that sits on my desk is waiting to be shaken once more; to be re-solved (resolved?) in a way that's necessarily different to what went before.

It's a puzzle.

But I love it—I love it a lot—and I can hold it in my hand as well as my mind's eye.

A good choice for the class, after all.

Who we are and what we do

In his book, *The Pleasures and Sorrows of Work,* Alain De Botton reflects on the intricacies of biscuit manufacture. He wittily observes the minute sub divisions of labour necessary for the launch of a new range of indulgent chocolate fancies, *Moments.* And he wonders, in the face of such absurdities, how we can possibly find meaning in the modern workplace.

De Botton's essay made me smile; almost certainly because the most successful humour plays on our sympathy with the objects of our laughter. His meditations rang true, not least because of the high-minded claims that pass for 'mission and purpose' in my own profession.

For years I told myself that distributing newspapers was a vital cog in the wheel of a diverse and pluralist democracy. Whereas these days, I passionately believe that newspapers—and especially the quality titles—tell us next to nothing of the truth. Worse, they present a veneer of facts, which (to stretch the metaphor) deter us from questioning the rather dodgy chipboard underneath.

Some years ago I attended one of those excruciating management sessions when you write down six words to describe yourself. My list went something like: father, painter, kayaker, climber, husband, thinker. My new boss asked, 'But what about work?' What about it? I replied. We didn't get on.

The more surprising outcome was that he was sacked and I prospered. A fact, which I like to think demonstrates that truth to yourself can sometimes—just sometimes—win out over bullshit.

In the world of Middle England's mid-size PLCs, defining ourselves by our professions is a pretty shallow existence. And yet, the higher up the corporate ladder we get, the more tempting it is to succumb. In much the same way that crap television and junk food provides us with instant, if temporary, gratification, our careers provide us with an easy and equally unsatisfying answer to the question of *'who we are and what we do.'*

As if by epilogue to these thoughts, I walked today along the green lane to Tretower. The house at its beginning is, I'm told, owned by Dick Renshaw, a famous climber, the first man to climb the South-east ridge of Dunagiri. A friend also told me he had taken up kayaking, paddling some of the hardest, if obscure, white water rivers in Wales. As we passed this morning, wooden sculptures were in progress in his garden.

I wondered if he had found meaning in his career—how indeed, he defined it—and whether, living aside a two thousand-year-old Roman Road, was inspiration to live more fully, or a cursed reminder of our own insignificance.

Gwaun

The Gwaun Valley tends to be overlooked by tourists: there are no obvious attractions, the access is difficult and the villages are, frankly, dour. And yet I like it a lot. We went there often when the boys were small, to walk by the river, pick blackberries or play in the water.

I returned today for the first time in a couple of years. We walked from Cilrhedyn Bridge to Llanychaer, the same route as always. It's not the most beautiful of walks, at least not by Pembrokeshire standards, and yet it has a rustic charm. The farms are worked hard, there are tyres in the fields, we found an abandoned tractor on the path today, the woodland is largely left to its own devices.

It seems the people of the Gwaun like doing things their own way. The valley is best known in Wales for celebrating *Hen Galan*, an alternative new year based on the Julian calendar—equivalent to our 13 January. The valley pubs reputedly pay scant regard to licensing laws on that day, or many others for that matter. As if to underline this individuality, one of its few well known farms is Penlan Uchaf, which promotes the unlikely combination of beef from long horn cattle and having a show garden for visitors. And at Llanychaer there is a garden which incorporates a flush loo, a metal sculpture of a miner (*or is it a farmer?*) and a kitchen range built into the wall!

But for me, the Gwaun is all about the river. The valley sides are steep, making for fast run off after rain, and streams swell the main flow at regular intervals. Today the river was dashing over gravel beds and churning through the falls. The trees on either bank grow down to the water's edge and our path crossed many rills running between their roots. Outside of the summer, it's not a walk for keeping your feet dry.

In winter, the river turns quickly to spate. I have kayaked it many times, and though never hard, it is not for the faint hearted. Below Llanychaer the river has carved a deep gorge, the walls of which are covered in rhododendrons. There is no way out, other than by boat, and though it is only a few miles to the sea, the water can't seem to wait; the rapids follow one after another, no eddies, no place to stop—until, more quickly than you expect, the last rush over cobbles into the harbour at Abergwaun.

It's somehow satisfying to finish a river journey at the sea. I have kayaked all over the world, including descents of major rivers in Asia and the Alps, but I can think of none with a more delightful ending than the Gwaun. The old harbour at Fishguard is one of the most picturesque in Wales; in the Sixties it was used as the film set for *Under Milk Wood*. And yet there is no attempt to cash in; no shops, no pubs, no commemorative plaques. So typical of the Gwaun, and one of the reasons I like it so much.

John Knapp Fisher

In the opening passage of his book, John Knapp-Fisher describes his approach to painting.

My work depends upon feeling for and involvement with the subject; the elimination of non-essentials, the use of pigment as an end in itself. That is, the quality of the painting or drawing must have a technical value regardless of the subject matter. These things cannot be dealt with by any rule of thumb.

These are wise words. Most serious painters will understand and have experienced what he means. Perhaps this is why I like his paintings so much, and have been collecting them, in a small way, for twenty years.

John lives and works from his studio in Croesgoch, only two miles from my house. He came here forty years ago and has gradually built his reputation so that he is now recognised as one of the finest painters in Wales. He is best known for dark, moody Pembrokeshire landscapes, often painted as nocturnes, the sky inked black and the buildings set like a stage—no coincidence he used to be a designer in the theatre.

But John's work has a much greater range. Though the style is always recognisable, he also paints townscapes, boats, the estuaries of Suffolk, the river Thames, and fish. Indeed, he's the best painter of fish I'm aware of and one of the few things I truly covet is one of his oil paintings of a mackerel or pollack.

My collection of his work is small—as are many of his paintings. I have half a dozen sketches and water colours, some of them painted before he came to Wales. I have some prints too—an easy present is always to buy me one of his images. And I have a stack of postcard reproductions, some of which I've framed. My father-in-law has a large original—I helped him chose it on the condition I could have it when he's gone—hopefully a long time yet.

Of course, I have a connection with the places John paints and this lies behind my interest, though not quite as you might expect. The vast majority of his subjects are within five miles of his studio and hence my house too. I find this inspiring; at a time when international travel has acquired an over-inflated status, it is worth reflecting that we can find a lifetime's creativity just by looking at what is around us. Sometimes we look too far and not close enough.

It's the sign of a good painting that we do not tire of seeing it. I enjoy my small collection and I enjoy visiting John's gallery to discover his latest work. Last weekend I called by and he enquired if I was still painting. He came to my exhibition a few years ago and I recall being delighted that he'd made the effort; I was pleased he'd remembered too. We chatted about the pictures he had on display—they were from his private collection; none were for sale.

I would not sell my paintings of his either, for they are an important reminder of the twenty or so years I've been in Wales. Indeed, they are an integral part of it. As John would put it—part of my feeling for and involvement in the landscape... with a technical value regardless of their subject matter... these things cannot be dealt with by any rule of thumb.

Hornet

Have you ever seen a hornet close to? I thought I had. My father used to claim he'd been stung by one—*right next to my eye*, he'd say, *like a dagger; could've blinded me.* If ever we saw a large wasp, to him it was a hornet; and as you do when you're a child, I believed him.

But this summer I saw one for real, in the woods at Somerford Common. It was hovering near a mound of straw, a nest of some kind with a small tunnel entrance. And it was huge—the hornet that is—this wasn't a large wasp, it was a golden, iridescent, gob-smacking monster. It's enormous, I kept saying aloud; absolutely bloody huge.

In truth, it was about the size of my thumb. But when you see something so wonderful and so unexpected, its presence distorts and focuses your perception. You'll have experienced something similar if you've ever photographed an animal in the wild, thinking it filled the viewfinder and yet the end result was a disappointing dot on the horizon.

And even if it had filled the frame, it could never be the same. That hornet is burned in my memory more surely and with more reality than any digital image. For a good few minutes, I watched it hover in and out of the entrance, moving forward and back, never changing its orientation, droning and buzzing like—well, a hornet.

The noise and size of hornets has led them to be misunderstood, feared even. Yet their sting is no more powerful than a bee, and they are far less likely to attack. It's a common occurrence for hornets and birds to share the same hollow tree. Though evidently, it's inadvisable to kill one near a nest as this releases pheromones that can disturb and 'anger' a swarm.

But who would want to kill such a fabulous creature?

This year I've seen some wonderful animals; I watched a Peregrine swooping over the cliffs at Ynys Barry, a million starlings massing at

Plumstone, a seal giving milk to its pup… and yet I reckon that hornet was the best by far.

My father was surely wrong. I don't doubt he was stung by something, but hornets don't reach as far north as Northumberland, and nothing we came across compared to what I saw this summer. I can still see it now: the plates of gold, the wings a-blur, the jewel in the straw…

God, it was huge.

West—where the light dies

Imagine how it would feel to lose your first born son. Worse, imagine him committing suicide; your golden boy kneeling into a noose, choosing death over any comfort you might offer. And as the tide of grief engulfed you, imagine learning that your partner and lifelong love has terminal cancer. Imagine she dies within a year.

The truth is I can't imagine how that would feel.

Sure, I can string some words together, probably clichéd—*curl up and die, cry my heart out*—but the reality is I have little conception of the visceral hurt, the psychological trauma such losses would bring. Those I've experienced seem trivial by comparison—or at least more natural and in their proper place. I have no idea what I would do; how I'd respond; where I would go.

My friend Jim Perrin faced these horrors, and more. And he went West—drawn to the Atlantic shores of Ireland, his instinct to reach out for the recuperative power of landscape. And he went, he writes in his book of the same name, because the West is the landscape of loss; because the West *is where the light dies*. But going West was as much a mental as a physical journey; in the landscape of Ireland he found not only solace, but also the strength to take the first faltering step out of grief's labyrinth.

West is an extraordinary book: beautifully written, heartfelt and times nauseating; it is poetic and scholarly, bawdy and funny; it is the story of unimaginable grief, a story we would never wish on ourselves. And yet it is also a love story; as much about life as it is about loss—if not exactly embracing his sorrow, he at least shows us the possibility of facing it, and even finding joy in our memories.

Because I know Jim and his story, I have thought a lot about his central theme of looking West. Is there something about *the West* I wonder, that draws us and provides solace for loss? In a literal sense, I think not, though I suspect Jim would counter that I am missing the importance of our myths and cultural subconscious. Perhaps, but to me it's as relevant that he turned to the sea. I was brought up on Tyneside, where the idea of Coast and East are synonymous—and yet the sea has always, in my mind, represented a place of escape, and to some extent of pilgrimage too.

But I agree with Jim in a broader sense. I agree that landscape, and wilderness in particular, has the power to heal, and also to reveal—often showing us to be stronger than we might imagine. Being 'in' the landscape is more than the journey or the view—it's about finding ourselves as much as finding the way; about looking inward as much as outward, and thereby glimpsing truths to which we are otherwise blind.

All my adult life I have climbed and walked and kayaked and cycled, often in extreme and wonderful landscapes; but I have done this as much for what I bring back to my 'normal life', as for the excitement or beauty that is always inseparable from any particular spot. Along the way I have found special places; places to which I habitually return. It is only conjecture, but if faced with a similar loss to Jim's, I suspect these are the places I would be drawn to.

Perhaps we each have our own West, it's position on the map less relevant than our memory, preferences, history… Jim's West may be more literal than mine, but then his need was more compelling, his life-journey more bereft. The triumph of his book is that it transcends the personal and introspective, to become something not only poignant but relevant to us all.

Ultimately, *West* is the story of how we might come through.

Interlude:
More than bugger all

I remember the first time I received a comment on my blog; the thrill that someone had taken the time to respond; the realisation that my writing wasn't lost in a virtual void.

That comment is still there to be seen—below a post dated January 2008. It was written by Sara Hudston, an author I knew and admired and now a regular Country Diarist for *The Guardian*. I'd been writing about Dylan Thomas and she mentioned there should be two Gs in Llareggub because it's derived from 'bugger all' spelt backwards. Which was is about as tactful a way of pointing out a typo to a friend as I know.

And I remember thinking, darn it! Who else might have spotted that mistake? I wondered also if the piece needed a picture? As it happens, I added one, and have done so for every post I've published since.

But more to the point, I owe a debt to Sarah, because I've been conscious ever since that the moment I press publish, what I've written is going out in the world for others to read and my reputation to stand by.

It's an exemplar too of how blogging as a writer requires us to pay attention to qualities that if we were writing only for ourselves we might have little or less reason to consider:

What title should I give this piece?

Is there a copyright needed for that picture?

What convention for speech marks should I use?

And remember to run that spellchecker!

Some of these are rather technical matters, and it would be misleading to suggest that every post needs to be perfect or that we should approach them all like an editor. But it's this awareness that what we write will be read by others that makes the difference between blogging and our notebooks—it requires us to consider not just 'you' but 'they'; to think like an author not a diarist.

It's one of those serendipitous coincidences that it was Sarah who wrote the first comment on my blog. For I owe her a related debt, this time from of a conversation we'd had some months prior. Sarah had written a book about my charismatic painting tutor John Skinner—it's beautifully crafted, and reading it was one of the inspirations for me to take up writing. I'm not sure I ever told her that, but I do recall us having a conversation in which she said, 'When your words go out in the world, they take on a life of their own—and you never know where they'll end up.' Sarah was referring to printed books and articles, but as I've come to learn, her wisdom is equally pertinent to blogging.

I'm forever surprised and delighted that my blog is read by others.

There's seldom a week goes by when a piece I've written doesn't throw up an unexpected connection—often years after pieces have been published. And there's no telling which or when it will be. Many of the posts I'm most pleased with have had the fewest of views; others have a reach and resonance that's baffling, but no less pleasing. One, which was name-checked by *The Times*, had tens of thousands of views that day, and later almost none.

But rather than responding to these surprises with a metaphorical (or even a physical) shrug of the shoulders, what this has taught me, is to always be attentive to what I publish.

You see, there's that P word again…

I've said it before, and I'll say it again and again—blogging is a form of publication—and what's more, unless you so choose, it doesn't go out print.

I write every post with the same care and attention that I'm giving to this piece, approaching my blog with exactly the seriousness and professionalism that I do articles in print, commissions I take and books or websites I've contributed to.

That's not to say that every post need takes hours to craft—though most of mine do—or that when starting out, you should think of every page as a pitch to an agent. There's balance to be struck, and a context to recognise. Blogs are not the same as academic articles or narrative fiction; there's an accepted style and a certain less formal approach (I'm generalising here, but I think fairly so) that can be refreshing and freeing—and superb practice for more traditional publication.

Anyone who's published a book, or written for a magazine will recognise the questions I posed above. I remember the first time I received a style guide and feeling somewhat terrified by the prospect. For if you're anything like me, it doesn't come naturally to be worrying about paragraph length and copyright, or even, for that matter, spelling and punctuation. (My school reports are peppered with the word 'careless'). But I've come to understand that being mindful of these details—the attention and the judgments involved—is vital to the practice of writing.

And what's more, I've come to love it because, despite the millions of posts that are frankly forgettable, there's scope for more serious work; for words that have been cared for and which we take the time to get right. In writing as bloggers, it's us who makes that choice.

Nearly fourteen years after first comment from Sarah I've still no real idea in what corners of the world my blogs will end up—whose eyes will read them; what difference they will make. And because of that—rather than despite it—I like to think that my writing is as good as it can be; that I've given it strength and wings enough to fly... that when I let it go free, it will have the chance of a life that's more than bugger all.

A new breed

I wonder if there is any greater display of eccentricity than the annual exhibition of the Amateur Entomologist Society? It's currently held at Kempton Park every October and attracts thousands of butterfly, beetle and stick insect enthusiasts. There's much tweed in evidence, a fair number of spotty youths with shortish trousers and many of all ages who could do with paying more attention to their personal hygiene.

Not that I fall into any of those categories, you understand.

But I must admit to being easily seduced by a fine display of hawk moths, and show me a perfect specimen of *Actias Luna* (don't worry, detail not really important) and my wallet is out before… well, before I've told Jane anyway.

I first went to the exhibition when I was eleven—in the days when it was held in Kensington. In some ways, not much has changed: the same interest groups (coleopterist, lepidopterists, dipterists) proudly manning the displays of their somewhat peculiar passions; the same collector types, drooling over second hand copies of *Wayside and Woodland Beetles* at £200; the same ruddy faced evangelicals promoting the 'bug club' for young entomologist.

I suppose there are fewer academic displays now (hardly any in fact); it's become more of trade show than a scientific gathering. But there were still gems that made me smile. Like the guy who announced to the crowd—*if anyone would like to know more about nematodes, I'll be free to give advice later.* Or the lady enquiring at the Watkins and Doncaster stand, Do you still have your shop in The Strand? *No madam, it closed before the War.* Pity, I was thinking of visiting for a moth trap…

But one difference was evident—a new breed of 'goth entomologists' threatening to usurp the resident nerds. The goth males were invariably in their late-teens or early twenties, resembling rejects from Games Workshop with multiple piercings, dagger tattoos and complexions that could do with more sun. Behaviourally, they made a bee-line (entomology pun there) for the spider and scorpion dealers, after which, having stocked up on nymphs and blowflies, they went looking for suitable mates.

And there appeared to be no shortage of females in black smocks— also with multiple piercings, dagger tattoos and complexions that could do with more sun. Judging by the number snogging in the grounds of Kempton Park, I'd say breeding conditions were excellent and a good time was had by all.

On reflection, I'm not sure they're really very different.

As I walked to the car, one of them was lying across the path, his head in a bush, groaning. *Excuse me?* I said testily, stepping over his Doc Martins and expecting a drunken grunt for my trouble. *Oh, I'm so sorry,* he replied in immaculate English... *It's fascinating in there: dozens of larvae in about their third instar I'd say, and some very interesting beetles too...*

I laughed all the way home.

Perhaps the play is not worth the candle

Yesterday I sent a piece of writing to a friend who's a well known and respected author. He was generous with praise and asked if I intended publishing the series I've been working on for the last few years.

It is significant that he didn't ask *if* I'd considered publishing; his emphasis was on whether or not I 'intended' to. I have no doubt that this subtle difference comes from his experience as a writer of, amongst other things, deeply personal biography.

For though I write about landscape and nature, these are usually a backdrop to the main subject: my relationship with my sons and the sense of wonder they've given me. Another writer friend once described my work as *an astonished journey into fatherhood*.

But therein lies a problem.

For that journey is inevitably a consequence of my own childhood and the fractured relationships I had with my parents—my father in particular. My father is dead, but to publish would inevitably cause hurt to others, my mother especially. I'm not, and never have been, the person she thinks I am—and she would not want me to improve her understanding. I have no wish to either.

Shortly after my first son was born, I recall Jane saying, *your trouble is that you have no reference points; or if you do they are the wrong ones.*

She was right. It took me years to realise that my sons might love me back. And when they did, that simple fact has driven my writing ever since.

But do my sons want their childhood 'out there' for others to read? And how would they feel about my interpretations of events? For interpretations is what they are. Though I strive to be honest, there is a necessary difference between objective and personal truth. Writers must always editorialise; the very act of pressing the keypad is an exercise choosing what to emphasise—and what not to.

I should explain that my work is never 'pour it all out' stuff—nor is it writing as therapy, from which dark secrets are revealed. It's simply a response to the situation I find myself in, and the past I came from.

But what of those who are close to either end of that *astonished journey*? I fear they might misinterpret my motives, question the need and argue the finer details—and in so doing, miss the bigger picture: which is that we can all come through.

And yet to write a book and keep it firmly closed, seems, if not exactly a pointless exercise, then a self-interested and self-limiting one. For I have learned from kayaking and climbing—as well as from fatherhood and writing—that for life to be worth living, we must take some risks with it too.

One in a million

Today, I returned to my house in Wales. When I arrived, I noticed there were crusty droppings on the floor, not unlike the body fluid that moths squirt if disturbed. Strange, I thought, to find these in December—and so many of them; on the window sills, the cupboard doors, the bathroom sink. I noticed too, some dusty marks on the ceiling and walls.

On the floor of my bedroom lay the body of the culprit. It was a young starling; I suppose it came down the chimney and become trapped, eventually dying from lack of food and water—perhaps from panic. It must have happened recently, for the body was soft and sleek; decay had not set in.

As I disposed of the corpse, it struck me what a beautiful bird the starling is. The feather pattern is a pearlescent blue-black, changing form and colour with the angle of the light. A starling's head is small with a dark green eye that in this case remained open, its beak dagger sharp, longer and more elegant than I realised. The whole body weighed no more than few ounces. It's wings opened one last time as I flung it into the field beyond my garden.

An hour later I stood under a million more.

Every evening in winter, up to two million starlings gather in a small copse of trees near my house. It's the largest roost in Wales, and an extraordinary sight to witness. People I tell about it, often ask if the birds swirl in fish-ball patterns, keen to hear of a spectacular aerial display. Sometimes the starlings do this, but more often, and especially when it's cold, they fly straight to the trees. This is not the disappointment it may seem.

For thirty minutes this evening the sky was black with their arriving; at one point they were literally brushing our heads, the din of their collective chattering like a river in spate. Amongst them flew buzzards, a sparrow hawk and evidently two goshawks had been there earlier. As the sun set over St Brides Bay, the silhouettes of the late comers were streaking against an orange and purpling sky.

To stand under that many birds is surprisingly beautiful. And what I realised tonight is that it is the closeness to them which makes it so. The swirling displays are spectacular when they occur, but usually they take place at a distance and at a remove. Like the bird I found in my house, it is the physical presence, the tactile sense of something beyond us, that best allows us to see the world differently.

What a strange but wonderful welcome home.

Sepia chapel

It's impossible to travel any distance in Wales without passing a chapel. As late as the early twentieth century, up to three quarters of the population attended nonconformist congregations; they're in every town and village, encompassing denominations from Methodist to Baptist to Presbyterian.

Recently, a friend sent me a picture of the chapel at Llangloffen near my house. Passing it today, you'd be forgiven for thinking little had changed. The farm which stands opposite is much the same too. It has a cobbled courtyard, a rookery, a look of run down despair.

But of course, the biggest difference is not the buildings, but the people—the throng of the congregation in that old photo, and not just in the way they dress. Had I taken a picture this Sunday there'd have been at most half a dozen cars and perhaps twice that in attendees. It's been said that most chapels are waiting for the last of their faithful to die before shutting the doors. Today there are fewer than 100 nonconformist ministers in Wales.

I can't complain; I don't attend and it's unrealistic to expect the organisations to keep them going. The communities that sustained these chapels, and the values that went with them, have gone or are disappearing. And it's important not to be sentimental too; sepia photographs give a sense of nostalgia but anyone reading the stories of Caradog Evans or Patrick O'Brian's first novel, *Testimonies*, would be warped to say that the society they depict was wholesome. Chapels, like all powerful institutions throughout history, had a dark side.

There are, of course, some iconic ones that are worth preserving. The chapel at Mwnt is an historic monument and the wonderful Soar y Mynydd is the exception that proves the rule about isolation and decline—it remains an active chapel despite the flooding of its catchment to create the Llyn Brianne dam. And I hope the Brynmawr chapel at Betws y Coed manages to keep going—for it was there, twenty years ago, that I married Jane on a day when it rained enough to launch an ark.

But the chapels of Wales are not quite dead yet. Many have been converted to houses, others taken over by Friends of the Friendless Churches; some have become craft centres, art studios, that sort of thing. And some continue as active congregations. On the day I visited Llangloffan there was a funeral taking place in nearby Mathry—the cars had filled the village, the approach roads were lined with pickups, one farmer opened his field for parking. I heard there were hundreds who couldn't get a seat.

I heard too that they'd sung the hymn, *Dyma Gariad Fel Y Moroedd*, Here is love, vast as the ocean.

Star party

I've written before about my youngest son's lack of interest in the natural world. For six years he's been captivated by trains, more recently his attention turned to *Star Wars*. Yesterday we were walking in Dyrham Park and a herd of deer sauntered past. *Look at those*, I shouted, pointing toward a stag with heavy antlers. He slashed his stick-cum-light-sabre in the general direction. *All dead*, he announced, *victory for Count Dylan!*

Last week, his interest in the intergalactic fantasy had given me an idea. It was a clear night, there was a full moon and Jupiter was displaying well too. *How about a star party?* I suggested. That would be fantastic, he replied, adding that he'd bring his blaster!

I used to have star parties with his brothers. They'd wrap up in coats and mufflers, stomping their feet as I set up the scope. And they'd stay outside for hours, becoming quite adept at finding planets, the Pleiades, the Andromeda galaxy or the Orion nebula. Now they're older and have girlfriends and other interests, they might not think it so cool. But they remember the basics and that's an excellent grounding for a teenager—the stars being the ultimate way to put things in perspective.

I don't understand the physics of astronomy, and can't properly comprehend the scale of it all. But in my own, very amateur way, I can find my way around the sky; I recognise the constellations and I know what should interest a seven year old boy. Technically, a full moon is not a good time to view, but when you're dealing with kids it's impressions that count. And by using a night sky application I knew that Jupiter's moons would be in line too.

It's astonishing what you can see with a reasonable telescope. Mine is an old Russian refractor that weighs a tonne—I remember the guy who sold it to me saying, 'It's good, if a bit agricultural.' He was right, but the light capture is enough to see the red spot on Jupiter, which in my book is pretty damn cool.

Dylan didn't agree. He was impressed that the moon was 240,000 miles away—but then asked, *is that as far as Wales?* When we got it in the viewfinder and I pointed out the craters, he asked if it was as big as the Millennium Falcon. And on finding Jupiter and showing him its four twinkling satellites, he said, *Do you think they're going to attack?*

Our party lasted all of five minutes.

After glancing again at Jupiter, he drank his milk, scoffed some cookies and wandered inside. I felt a bit deflated. But then, you never know what knowledge they're storing away. For tonight, when I put him to bed he asked... *You know in Star Wars; when they go to the death star...* Yes, I replied, feigning interest. *Because I was thinking if the moon is far away and Jupiter is ten times further and galaxies are a million times more—then how do they do it?*

'I don't know,' I said; but you're getting there slowly, I thought.

Cwm Idwal

If I was forced to pick a single place that meant more to me than any other, Cwm Idwal would be a high contender. It's in the Ogwen Valley, a few hundred feet above the main road to Bethesda, on the path to Twll Du, the Devil's Cauldron and Glydyr Fawr mountain. The Cwm is a hanging valley, glacial in origin and now a protected site of natural interest with particularly rare plants including the Snowdon Lilly

It's also of interest to mountaineers—the Idwal Slabs have provided an introduction to thousands of novice climbers and the surrounding cliffs are home to many test pieces, including the aptly named Suicide Wall. Years ago I climbed these routes and can still picture the individual moves, the precarious belays and the long loose descent into the gully to the side of the rocks.

I remember the day we found a rose wedged in a crack, with a note from a girl whose boyfriend had died in the Himalayas. It made Jane cry. We were there to go climbing but came back despite the sunshine—somehow, it didn't seem right.

And I remember too, the afternoon of our wedding day, when we walked to the Cwm in pouring rain and held each other on the rock where we'd kissed three years previous, and known it was more than an office romance.

We've been back many times since. The other year we took our boys and stood on the same rocks as they turned away in embarrassment—*yuk* they said!

That's teenagers for you. But then one day they'll probably be old romantics just like their father. And if they are ever inclined to kiss a girl in a magical place, then Cwm Idwal will still be there, waiting and as wonderful as ever.

Tag Heuer watch

It's a sign of age to have a receipt box that's overflowing—indeed, it's probably a sign of age to have one at all. These days most invoices are electronic, but I still keep the habit of filing the paperwork for those items I perceive to be of value. This morning, I spent a pleasant half-hour rooting through the records for bikes I bought thirty years ago, jewellery that's even older, and paintings from a lifetime of collecting.

But try as I might, I couldn't find the receipt for my TAG Heuer watch.

I know I bought it sometime in the late Eighties, the first (and only) expensive one I've ever purchased. From memory, it cost me about a thousand pounds, but I think that must be wrong, which was why I was checking the file. It seems too much to have paid—a lot of spare cash for the time—I'd not buy a watch for that now.

And yet, for the last ten years it's languished in a drawer. The face has tarnished so the battery must have leaked; the diving bevel no longer turns and the strap could do with an extra link or two. All in all, it's in a rather sorry state. Which is a pity for an item that holds memories much richer than any receipt could record.

TAG Heuer watches were once all the rage among kayakers. Mine came with me on expeditions to Nepal (twice), Turkey and several trips to the Alps. It's been down more rivers and across more stretches of sea than any boat I've owned. I wore it when I was married and as a surprise wedding gift bought Jane a matching one that she still wears today.

I wonder if there's any other object that accompanies us as much as the watches we wear?

A wedding ring perhaps, but they're essentially passive—whereas a watch is something we use, a party to the decisions we take. How many times did I check the face of my TAG Heuer; how many choices did I confirm—or cancel—on the turning of its hands? How much water did it witness flowing under the bridge of my life?

The model I have is a Formula 2000, which reflects TAG Heuer's sporting image. The company has been an official timekeeper at events dating back to the 1920 Olympics; they're a sponsor today of sports as diverse as football, sailing and athletics. It's all nonsense, of course—part of their lifestyle branding—for in practice, any digital watch is more than accurate enough, and I doubt there's an athlete (or a kayaker) who'd still use a model like mine.

But precision's not the point anymore, just as it never really was. Watches—and certainly ones of this sort—have always been about more than utility. For many, they're a form of conspicuous consumption, as anyone who's passed through the arrivals hall at Geneva airport will understand. For others, they're about fashion and style, a statement of who we are—or more likely, who we'd like to be.

The strange thing is, none of this has ever appealed to me. We need to be careful in assessing ourselves, but I reckon I don't risk a hostage to fortune if I say that I'm not a brash or bling person—nor for that matter a style guru. And as for sporting prowess, what little there was is now almost as dormant as my watch this last decade.

Which makes me think, it's about time I recharged the batteries. Coming to the end of this interminable standstill, there's something pleasing about the idea of its hands turning once more. Wearing it would be a symbol of new beginnings and times gone by—a reminder that all our days are precious.

So I'm going to send it to a specialist repairer. No doubt the cost will be more than is sensible, but maybe that's fitting. For its value lies not in money but in memories—and in the making of new ones.

And that's an asset that takes time to grow.

Cutting back

Last spring I was preparing for a bike ride that would take me across the UK from Aberystwyth to Great Yarmouth. And on my training route, I'd always cycle a particular lane—it had the most fabulous hedges, all overgrown and shady and bursting with wildlife. I saw a bullfinch there in March, a hare lolloping down a side track, brimstone butterflies right into summer—when I returned in the autumn the hedge was heavy with sloes.

On Saturday I was back on my bike, starting my training for another charity ride. I was looking forward to that lane; indeed, as I approached it I was thinking how, when passing through much of the middle of England, it was the hedgerows I'd liked the best. Throughout the ride, there'd been pretty much a direct correlation between bushes and birdsong—I remember commenting as much to one of my colleagues.

As such, I was in a light frame of mind as I pressed on the pedals and into Common Road, under a sharp cerulean sky. The day before there'd been goldcrests in my garden, long-tailed tits on the silver birch and a blackcap on the forsythia. Warmer weather was hinting at spring—perhaps that bullfinch—or a flock of yellowhammer—would be there again?

Not only were they not, but my mood had changed within a few hundred yards.

Some people might think it strange that a bit of hedge trimming could conjure any sadness. After all, it's only a few gnarly trees—overgrown bushes really—and it can be good for certain species if the lanes are kept in order. What's more, doesn't pruning make the trees more robust in the long run?

It's true that it makes the hedgerows thicker. And cutting back every few years, is probably better for wildlife than annual trimming. For every summer of growth, it's estimated two additional bird species will come to nest—so cutting less frequently is a good idea. On the other hand, there are butterflies which only lay eggs on new growth and many birds prefer low hedges—for these species, regular trimming is what's needed. The ideal is to prune every three years in careful rotation, ensuring no area is reduced too severely at any one time.

But all that was clearly too much hassle for the farmer on Common Road. I reckon it was ten years since he last cut those hedges (ironically quite good)—and when the time came that something had to be done, he wasn't going to be worried about the niceties of yellowhammers or bullfinches. Judging by the results of his mechanical flail I don't reckon he's bothered about much in nature at all. He's not only cut the thinner growth, he's slashed the nearby trees, splintered the blackthorn into shards, even smashed his own fences. In all, he reduced the hedge by over six feet.

I know most of it will grow back; I know that Common Road isn't a conservation imperative, and I know it probably looks worse than it is. But there's something quite brutal about all of this. Something that doesn't feel right—a sense that with just a little more care, it would have made such a difference.

As it is, there'll be less birdsong on my training rides this spring, and I guess this autumn I'll be going elsewhere for sloes.

Why exactly are we doing this

It was raining—hard as it happens—the traffic crawling and a snake of tail lights extending somewhere towards Birmingham. The kids were moaning in the back; the iPad was out of charge and the crisps weren't the right sort. Driving 300 miles up the M6 on a Friday night is not the time or place to be impatient...*Remind me again, why exactly are we doing this?* snapped Jane.

Five hours later we reached Preston and our hotel for the night. *If we get up at six*, I jollied, *we could reach the Lakes in a couple of hours, have breakfast in Keswick...* Jane's look suggested I keep schtum.

But it's strange how moods can turn. The room was spotless, the pub next door just what we needed, and Dylan slept through without a murmur. Next morning we were off at eight-thirty, driving to Penrith under a cobalt sky and debating how we might lengthen the walk in.

Our goal was Black Sail Hut, one of the oldest youth hostels in the UK and certainly, the most remote. It's situated in the Ennerdale Valley and requires a five mile trek from almost any direction. Travelling with us was a friend and her two young children, which explains why our sacks were bulging with sweets and chocolate as we strolled the south shore of Buttermere, heading for Scarth Gap.

Now Scarth Gap isn't exactly a huge pass; it's one of the tourist routes up Haystacks Mountain and takes about an hour for an averagely fit walker. But when you're six or seven years old, and playing with your mates, it's a different prospect. It's steep too, and the boys took to holding a stick between them, shouting as they hauled themselves up the rocky path; *one and two and three and four...* I smiled, for they were counting steps, as if parodying the title of my book (that's not a contrived plug—it really happened), and I marvelled at how life so often repeats itself.

By the time we reached the last rise, Dylan and young Jack (so small I could almost fit him in my pack) were a hundred yards ahead, waving their poles and posing for photographs. The descent to the hut took half the time and twice as many stumbles—we arrived mid-afternoon, dumped our coats, put on a brew and sat listing to the mountains.

An hour or so later, the wardens arrived; they'd been to the pub they said, over at Wasdale Head.

I must have looked puzzled.

It's only a forty minute fell-run they explained, pointing to the pass by Pillar Rock. I noticed their stick-thin limbs, their sinewed calves—and estimated their combined body mass index to be approaching half of mine! They were great wardens though—proper mountain people—and it was obvious they cherished the time they were here.

Black Sail is also unique amongst the remoter UK hostels in that it provides evening meals. Dinner was soup, sausage casserole and sticky toffee pudding, washed down with Cumbrian Ale and a bottle of red. Another family was staying too and by the time the stars were out there was one conversation around the wood-burning stove and a shared sense of how special this place is.

So, having driven three hundred miles, then walking another five to sleep in a shepherd's hut, we woke the next morning and promptly walked back. There was mention of severe weather approaching, but the sun held out. As did the little ones, who, though tired, still managed to reach the pass before me. Ninety minutes later we all were back at the car and soon heading to Keswick for lunch before the long drive south.

There are few places in England that can offer such a compact adventure as Black Sail. Of course, walking to the Ennerdale Valley doesn't risk life and limb—but it's a world away from the clutter and comfort of everyday life. It's part of the comprehensive education I want for my children, in the hope they'll learn to appreciate and participate in nature—to understand there's more to life than Gameboys and cinema and, for that matter, Premier Inns or swanky hotels.

It's to the YHA's great credit that it keeps Black Sail running. I wish the Association would find and open others like it, for I'm sure the demand would be there.

We drove home in less time than it had taken to reach Preston on Friday night. Tired, yes, but more refreshed and more ready for the week ahead than if we'd called it off.

Remind me again, Jane had asked on our way north, *why exactly are we doing this?* As we unpacked the car two days later, Dylan begged, *Next time we go—could we stay a bit longer?*

    Enough said.

Badgers

Sometimes, if we see the most ordinary of things in an unexpected context it can jolt our senses. I was once transfixed on the train journey to London by a woman flossing her teeth in the carriage—she nonchalantly rinsed her mouth with spring water, spitting into a plastic bag whilst chatting to her friends! Another time—again on a train—I was travelling through Germany and I remember being shocked by the workmen drinking steins of lager with their breakfast.

All of which is a contrived introduction to the surprising circumstance in which I last saw a badger.

It was shuffling across the scrubby cliffs on the approach to St David's Head. I was there at midday and had passed Porth Melgan cove when I saw it—in truth, the badger wasn't so much shuffling as scurrying, covering the ground at a pace I've not seen one move before.

Badgers are relatively common in Pembrokeshire. There are numerous setts in the lanes near my house, though a good sighting is still infrequent enough to make a comment if not exactly stop the car. Most times we spot one it's caught in the headlights—if we see one in the daylight, it's invariably road-kill.

One spring, a young cub took to visiting our garden and we'd peek between the curtains to watch it sniffing for worms on the lawn. Lit by the glow of the street lamps, it reminded me of those nature watch programmes that set up hidden cameras to film cubs feeding at night—badgers were considered special then, and in many ways they still are, though recent increases in numbers have led to fears of a link to bovine TB and the threat of culls.

I don't know about the science but I find the prospect of culls rather sad. We have so few wild mammals and these sturdy creatures seem to me to be symbolic of a widely held feeling that our countryside shouldn't all be lost to industrial agriculture. How anyone could ever find sport in baiting them is beyond me—thankfully, that's been illegal for a long time.

Watching the badger scurry away, it looked rather comical—hunched and dwarfish, its stubby legs racing to catch up with an elongated snout. I learned recently that badgers are related to weasels. I'd not seen the resemblance before, but there's a vague familiarity in the head shape, though the gait of the one I saw didn't suggest the cunning we associate with its smaller cousins.

Badgers, like weasels now I come to think, have long been anthropomorphised in stories, often as trusty stalwarts, as in *The Wind in the Willows*. In that book, the weasels and stoats are the bad guys, ending up on the wrong end of Badger's cudgel! If I were writing in that fashion, I reckon my badgers would be rugby forwards: a touch dim on first impression, but single-minded and built for their task—absolutely necessary too, for all that we don't notice or appreciate them enough.

Returning to my encounter, it had never occurred to me to look for badgers on the coast path. I suspect the one I saw had wandered a little too far for comfort, hence its haste to reach the flatter ground. But why wouldn't they be there? Beyond the head is a wide expanse of moor, plenty of places for a deep sett, and a deal less interference from farmers or car headlights.

The strange thing about these encounters is how they affect our returning. Every time I pass through Didcott station I remember that woman flossing her teeth; I still have an entirely unreasonable preconception that all German workmen drink beer with their breakfast! And the next time I visit St David's Head I shall look for badgers on the off chance—I doubt I'll see them often, but it won't really matter. Sometimes, the knowledge they are there is enough.

The role of the countryside in a crisis

The events of the early stages of the pandemic will be with us for decades. Economically, there'll certainly be pre and post Covid eras, and socially, though evidence shows we swiftly revert to our norms, most commentators expect there to be some adjustment. I wonder, though, as I reflect on the 'Stay Away' sign that's appeared in a lane near my house, at the deeper changes this shock to the system will bring, and the attitudinal legacies it may leave.

Somewhat to my surprise, I've coped well with the restrictions of the lockdown. I suppose that being an introvert, I was always going to be less affected by the lack of social interaction than I was by the limits to getting outdoors. In the event, I've adapted to that too, finding new ways to explore, making a virtue of what's local; *dwn ei filltir sgwar*, as they say in Wales—a man of his own square mile.

But for all that I've found solace on my doorstep, there's also been sadness—not in the landscape or the shrinking of my horizons, but in narrow minded insularity which the sign in that lane so typifies. Walk two miles from where I'm writing this and you'll find others of similar ilk: Stay Home, Caravans not Welcome, No access—the internet is awash with much the same and worse.

Fear, of course, feeds our darker instincts. In the first grip of a pandemic (that very word is so emotive) we want action that keeps us safe—we don't care about fancy-pants reasoning or the niceties of whether this or that restriction offends against our individual rights. And actually, I agree. Over sophistication would risk undermining the core message—especially when there are sections of society who seem to be determinedly irresponsible and selfish.

But that doesn't mean, we shouldn't call out attitudes and behaviours that in any other context we'd be quick to condemn. Of course an urban exodus to Tenby or Pen Y Fan should not be encouraged—and those who flout the rules should rightly be penalised. But when the call to stay at home starts to morph into a more general 'outsiders not welcome' then we risk crossing a line. Last week, the tires of suspected 'visitors' cars were slashed in communities across Wales; there were farmers calling for footpaths to be closed, there were people posting pictures of suspiciously parked vehicles, and there were keyboard warriors glorying in the Easter stay-away, not as a regretfully necessary measure, but as a statement of neo-tribal identity.

If this were just a few individuals then perhaps I could shrug it off. But regretfully, some of those who should know better have acted poorly too. The posts on social media by the Pembrokeshire National Park for example—with their sideways digs at caravaners and second homeowners—are ill thought-through, reinforcing an undercurrent of 'us' and 'them' that no afterthought of 'you'll be welcome when it's over' can ever mitigate. In part, that's because it isn't going to be 'over'—at least not for a long while, and not in a clean-cut way.

The real sadness in all this is that rural areas have, at least potentially, an important role to play in helping us come through what will be a messy and imperfect emergence from this crisis. If we think of those few environments that can relatively safely allow for exercise, wellbeing, families being together, then the outdoors must come high on the list. In a week when it was reported that the Government is considering the restarting of construction projects on the basis that working outside poses a limited risk, then surely walking or mountaineering or surfing or sailing… must be even less so.

On Thursday there was some clarification that the current legislation allows for a short drive of up to five minutes in order to take a much longer period of exercise. To many, myself included, this makes a huge difference to their horizons—and ultimately their mental health. We should welcome the clarity rather than feigning confusion or retreating to the comfort of inflexible prescriptions. For these are exactly the types of baby steps we will need, helping us to move beyond slogans without compromise to safety or leaping from one extreme to another. I'd like to see our National Parks (and other similar bodies) start thinking and communicating along similar lines, rather than promoting the blanket closure of our precious natural resources.

But most of all, I'd like to see a change in an underlying attitude of 'us and them', which if not universal is worryingly to the fore. Those of us lucky enough to live in rural areas—and especially those with the ability to influence others—must come to terms with the reality that there will inevitably be some risk from visitors arriving from the city, just as those in urban areas are now taking daily risks to supply us with food and medicine and telecoms and building materials... We live in an interconnected and mutually dependent society and the idea that it's 'our' local health service or 'our' landscape or 'our' footpaths or that these regional assets are most definitely 'not yours', is not only wrong in its reasoning, it's shabby in sentiment and, actually, bad for our future too.

Last week I was struck by a simple Facebook post from my friends at Alpine Action Adventures—they were offering key workers a substantial discount on any holiday they might take this or next year. Sure, it's a marketing device; but what a fantastic and creative gesture. They have other offers too and are responsibly encouraging guests to think ahead without the need to risk large deposits or inflexible commitments. What they are saying is 'Come and stay, we're grateful for what you've done; we're happy to share some of our good fortune'— and these are people who live in France! Let's have more and similar gestures from businesses and public bodies here in the UK.

My grandfather, who lived through the great depression, was fond of the saying, 'we reap what we sow'. These too are seminal times, and we should grant some leeway for the planting of a few bad seeds. But in a few short months, the communities and the landscapes of rural Wales will have a golden opportunity to show—and share—the depth of their value to us all. In so doing, they can make a huge contribution to our national wellbeing and play a vital role in shaping some of the few positive legacies of this pandemic. Rather than putting signs on gates (either literally or online) we ought—right now—to be thinking of how we might embrace that challenge, even if the ways to do so are not immediately obvious.

INTERLUDE:
KEEPING ON

At the age of 85, the Nobel prize winner, José Saramago, started a blog, writing an average of one post every two days for a year. They were subsequently published as The *Notebook* which is, ironically for an online medium, now out of print, albeit easily sourced on the Internet. I'd recommend you get hold of a copy.

Saramago writes with such urgency that reading his posts is a lesson in getting swiftly to the point. They're instructive too in the practice of writing for the form, the variety and freedom blogging affords—and indeed demands—if we're to maintain interest for ourselves and our readers. His posts begin on a polemical note, many of them critical commentaries of George W Bush, Berlusconi and the politics of his native Portugal. But as the year unfolds, I noticed how his interests widened and while returning often to the themes of injustice and corruption, he diverts us into reflections on music, poetry, dreams, religion, the lifecycle of a flower…

It seems to me that these rhythms and flows are essential to nurturing any blog of the sort that reflects on life and the world. Focusing on one subject is not only monotonous for the reader, it sets up demands that are likely unsustainable for the writer too. In 'keeping on' we should be conscious that writing a blog is a marathon not a sprint—and be mindful that the reason so many runners give up is in their setting too demanding a schedule, only to burn out with boredom, fatigue and inevitable injury.

I know, because I've been there.

Look at any manual for runners and you'll find recommendations for pacing and distance, sprints and endurance, road and cross-country. This is the athletic equivalent of what artists call theme and variation, the practice of modifying a motif in ways that play with its form and content—a sort of shuffling of the deck that allows the game to begin again.

And as with the playing of cards, we are best to start slowly, learning the patterns and tactics, until eventually playing our hands at speed. We can master several games too, adding variety of a different sort.

But enough of metaphors. What does this tangibly mean for the writing of our blogs? How, practically, do we develop the themes and variations without them becoming a random selection of trivia or narcissisms? And how do we connect to our central concerns with the fresh perspectives and enthusiasm that keep our writing alive?

The best answer I have is practice.

It's often said it takes 10,000 hours to master a skill. The hypothesis, which was famously proposed by Malcolm Gladwell in his book *Outliers,* has been widely criticised as an over-generalisation. That may be so, but it remains the case that posting regularly is essential to developing a feel for your blog and acquiring the abilities to write on a variety of topics. More than that, blogs thrive on regularity—if posts become too infrequent then readership will fall and along with it, our purpose and motivation.

Some bloggers keep a rolling list of ideas, finding it helpful to jot down potential posts and even schedule their publication. And because blogs often integrate photographs, scanning our camera rolls and bookmarking pictures can trigger memories and spark inspiration too.

In this respect, blogging is no different to other forms of writing, for which the keeping of notes becomes an essential part of habitual good practice. I realised early on that I tended to file too many ideas in my head only to recall them when the moment had passed. There's now no end of journaling and other creative applications that can integrate notes with blog platforms. But most often I use my smartphone or a jotter—and come to think of it, the contrast in those technologies would make a good hook for a post.

I'd caution, though, against 'live blogging' in the manner of social media platforms such as Facebook or Instagram. It's perfectly possible to upload 'on the go' and very occasionally it can work well (my friend Michelle who writes a garden blog will post 'live' from events like Chelsea and Hampton Court flower shows), but if we are blogging primarily as writers, then our purpose, in the main, requires us to be more reflective and particular with our words.

An editorial technique I've unconsciously adopted is to punctuate more topical posts with less immediate themes which give me a structure to work within, rather than always searching for something new. This book includes several examples: the objects of life, past imperfect; nature, collections… I think of these as something akin to the regular columns we read in magazines and newspapers. Far from being repetitive, they add another layer to the complexity of theme and variation that's part of the skill in curating a blog.

The word curate means to select or organise, typically in an expert capacity. And thinking in this way—applying what I've consistently described as a professional approach—is part of the joy, and benefit, of blogging. It's one of the reasons why I'm less keen on platforms like Medium or Substack, which provide an outlet but not a home for your writing.

All of the mainstream blogging platforms are formatted to showcase the latest posts on a landing or home page, but they also have the capacity for fixed pages, galleries and archives. These help to organise content into topics rather than chronology, and direct those who might want to read more on a particular theme. Subject tags can be applied to posts too, though again I'd advise some restraint. Blogs with 200 labels are as good as saying there are no meaningful divisions to speak of; much better to have a well chosen selection, with a search box for those readers who want to delve deeper.

There are myriad other ways to vary and curate our blogs: posting pictures once a week; noting anniversaries, writing reviews, featuring guest posts… It's also helpful to remember that not every post needs to be startling, and that over time and with practice we (and our readers) can feel our way to the form and content and frequency that's sustainable for our taste. If one of the delights of blogging is that we never know where our words will end up, it's equally true that they can also be deleted and amended if needs be. To use a cliché: 'not making the perfect an enemy of the good' is an integral part of caring and keeping on.

Today, as I conclude these notes, it is the July 6 and, out of curiosity, I turned to that same date in José Saramago's notebook. His post was a response to a review of his blogging and a claim that he wasn't a proper proponent. The piece is short and imperfect; it could do with some editing and paragraph breaks. And yet within a few hundred words it moves from acknowledgement of his shortcomings to a discussion on the levels of analysis and appropriate indignation a blogger might express. Are there any limits to the later, he asks?

The following day Saramago leaves these considerations behind; shifting his subject to conscience and identity as a writer. The next he writes a beautiful reflection on his adoptive land, the sense of time passing and a search for lost youth. Soon after he reflects light heartedly on politics and then lists his recommendations for summer reading. Not every post is sparkling, and as standalone pieces, they might struggle to capture our interest. But collectively, whether he's conscious of it or not, they shape into a coherent journey for the reader; a shining example of trusting in our words and having confidence in what we have to say.

And that, it seems to me, is the essence of keeping on.

Whippet life

How often do we make choices which for one reason or another turn out to be especially delightful? By definition, it can't be very often—and in my experience, there's precious little relationship to price, importance, or even the level of prior thought. If you're anything like me, you'll have made as many well-planned and expensive mistakes, as you have snap decisions that turn out to change your life.

The best purchase I ever made was a tumbledown cottage, for which I paid what would now be the price of a new hatchback car. It's not for any profit that I'm pleased (I doubt there's any after all the renovation cost), but for the family nexus it's become, the joy we've had, the memories and friendships it holds... And not least, for the chance encounter that led to my most recent and most constant of companions.

I'd long wanted a whippet. For years I used to draw cartoons of them in my diaries, hiding a caricature version into humorous sketches of the places we'd visited. Finding the dog in the picture became a bit of a trademark, for all that our own at the time was a Jack Russell terrier.

She left us more than ten years ago. A farm-bred ratter, she'd been fine with the older boys but when Dylan arrived her instincts reverted to type. After the third biting incident we moved her on to a family with teenagers and, to be honest, I was pleased to see her go. The prospect of another dog had seldom been discussed.

Until last year—when we passed a couple on the coast path with the most beautiful brindled whippet. I couldn't but stop and admire him, and when we learned he'd just sired a litter, Jane quickly asked for their number... for the future, she claimed... we'll have a think, I said... and maybe be in touch, she added.

Sooner rather than later.

That evening, Jane nagged me to phone, the next day we viewed the pups, and less than 24 hours after that chance encounter, we'd reserved the smallest dog in the litter. Oscar, born on St David's day, would be with us in five weeks' time. Later that evening, the UK announced its first nationwide lockdown...

And for the next month all we did was walk lanes, read books and research whippet facts to help us count the days.

As I look back now I wonder what on earth we thought we were doing? It can't be sensible to buy a dog that quickly; even knowing the commitment I should surely have insisted we reflected for longer. The money's not the issue; it's the cost to your lifestyle, the responsibility, the getting up every morning... Stories of lockdown puppies are all over the internet—portents for all to read.

But logic isn't always our best pilot. And if you knew how hard I find it to declare that, you'd have some idea of the delight I've found in my little friend. You might have noticed the change from 'our' to 'my' in that last sentence. For almost a year he's barely left my side, growing up and growing closer—and quicker too. Which was why I'd wanted a whippet in the first place; the fastest dogs on the beach, I used to say.

And now mine is.

Yesterday we were up at dawn with the sand to ourselves. We walked three miles without much of a sound but for waves and the occasional whistle. Owners often talk of their dog's love and loyalty, as if they had human emotions; they chat to them too, though knowing they can't understand. I do the same. But really, the bond is one of 'co-presence': an unspoken companionship that's beyond any words—or for that matter, reason.

Oscar doesn't do logic either and in a way that's why we care for our pets so much.

What he does do is run like the wind, return when I call and wag when I rise every morning. Three miles on the beach today, hundreds more every month; how many steps will we take together? Jane and Dylan love him too; he's the best family dog we've had by far. They both say they knew it would work; that they sussed it (and me) in seconds; that their hearts, not their heads told them what to do.

They're right of course, in that sometimes—just occasionally, mind you—it's fine to take a flier.

Of birds and worms and other beasties

My wonderful work colleague Kerrie, has a fear of birds. *Like the dead reincarnate*, she described them today, adding that she'd had to turn away from watching *Frozen Planet* because she couldn't stand the penguins. *Those horrible pecking beaks, brrrr… they're evil.* We laughed at the ridiculousness of her phobia, but it's real to her nonetheless.

Jane doesn't like worms; she goes cold at the thought. So, of course, our older boys delight in throwing juicy ones around the garden, while she takes cover in the shed. Meanwhile, Dylan dreams up dishes like worm spaghetti and thinks there's little more amusing than hiding a few in her handbag.

Phobias are common—in the last few day I've had various comments from blog followers admitting to a dislike of moths, spiders and the like. They differ from rational fears in that we know they're unfounded. For example, I'd be scared if I found a tiger in my bedroom—that's rational because it might eat me! But I'm not (irrationally) worried that if I went upstairs now, there'd be one lurking in the ensuite.

Thankfully, I don't suffer from nature terrors—unless you count acute embarrassment at the prospect of dancing in public. I'm wary of horses and cattle, but that's not phobic in the true sense. And I wouldn't want to eat slugs, but again, that's not the same as considering birds to be the *dead reincarnate*. In fact, I often spend time imagining what small animals would be like if they suddenly grew—as a friend said to me recently, *imagine a six-foot stoat!*

I was about to end this piece by asking what your fear or phobia might be. But then I remembered my stroll with Jane last night—we were passing a wooded area of town and she admitted, *I wouldn't like to walk here alone.*

Neither would I, and it put me in mind that the animal I most fear, irrationally or otherwise, is my very own species.

Politics and philosophy—a lesson in two parts

Just over forty years ago I went to university to study politics. It was around the time when Margaret Thatcher and Ronald Reagan were first elected; unemployment was high, the Soviet Union remained a threat and, in my final year, reports from Afghanistan and the Falklands glued us to the TV in the Students' Union bar.

Academic politics is primarily the study of power: the ways it's structured in a world of nation-states and how they interact on the international stage. Whereas most of my fellow students preferred the classes on government and international relations, I was drawn to the philosophical side, which looks not so much of how things 'are', as to how they 'ought' to be.

This distinction between the 'is' and the 'ought' is bread and butter stuff to philosophers—it's precisely the point of the exercise in topics such as ethics and justice which became my subsidiary subjects. By the time I graduated, these were my chief interest and though many friends and family asked if I'd thought of going into public affairs, I understood by then that the two sides of the political coin have very little in common.

In the years since leaving university, I've cultivated a certain disdain for politics and its proponents. Ironically, given my career in newspapers, I hold much the same view of the media too. For several years I actively stopped reading or viewing any news reports, and still today I'm deeply sceptical of the stories that are served up as fact. The prospect of being involved in the political merry-go-round, even on a minor campaigning basis, has remained about as attractive as the warm milk we were forced to drink at junior school—the removal of which I regard as Margaret Thatcher's best ever decision!

Or at least that was the case until the coronavirus crisis and the monstrous restriction of our civil liberties that continues to be imposed under the guise of public safety. My use of the word 'monstrous' will make clear how I regard the extended lockdown here in Wales. It's a visceral thing, a sense that just 'is' within me, as much as something I 'ought' logically to feel—and although I could set out all the arguments here, that's not the point of this piece.

What's relevant is that for the first time in my adult life, I've become a letter writer, a tweeter, a commentator of Facebook. I've followed every Welsh politician that matters (to be fair that's not many) and bombarded them with questions; I've signed petitions, written to newspapers, sought out data and read the legislation and scientific advice in full. The National Parks have governance websites that allow you to read their policies—and like me, complain at their closure of huge areas of the countryside and general kowtowing to the wishes of their paymasters.

In part, I've done this by way of experiment. I wanted to see what difference—however small—I might make. If I campaigned hard enough, might anybody actually listen? Along the way, I've learned some of what works and what doesn't—when to challenge and when to stop—which posts get the most likes, and which are more likely to fall on deaf ears. At times it's almost exhilarating. I can see how some might find a purpose in this as a profession.

But most of all I've learned the process is exhausting. In fact, it feels like the intellectual equivalent of banging your head against a wall in the hope that someone takes pity on your cries. The reason for this is that success has absolutely nothing to do with winning the intellectual argument. Indeed, I should remove 'winning' from that last sentence— for it's now clear to me that political campaigning has almost nothing to do with intellectual honesty at all.

The historian Michael Ignatieff made this point in an interview, reflecting on his time as leader of the Liberal Party of Canada. Ignatieff is a formidable thinker and yet he described how all the skills he'd acquired—and had thought would be helpful—were of little or no use in the political arena. In politics, the protagonists have an agenda which they pursue regardless of consistency or intellectual merit—those concerns are the niceties of losers. What matters to lobbyists and politicians is simply to prevail—and if that means you need to pivot your reasoning or ignore some inconvenient truths, then so be it.

Dominic Cummings wouldn't be concerned—from 'Taking Back Control' to 'Get Brexit Done' he's become the embodiment of a political method that's based on little more than the repetition of populist messages—ideally wrapped in slogans which capture the sentiment but suppress any critical thought. The recent calls to 'Stay Home, Save Lives and Protect the NHS' are more benign but little different in their veracity. In a distressing reversal of the academic distinction we began with, politics in practice has evolved into the art of promoting a partisan view of what 'ought' regardless of the truth of what actually 'is'.

But was it ever any different?

Forty years ago the slogan on billboards across the UK was 'Labour isn't Working'. It's now famous as the Saatchi and Saatchi campaign which led to the Conservative victory in 1979. And yet if you look carefully, you'll see that the line of supposed benefit-seekers is actually the same twenty people—all of them volunteers—from the Hendon Young Conservatives, photographed from different angles. What's even more ironic is that by the end of Thatcher's first term in office, unemployment had more than doubled.

That's a long time ago—and no doubt we'll look back on this crisis and its impact on civil liberties in a different light too. But for now, I'm done with campaigning, the toll on my wellbeing is too great. Indeed, the prospect of civil disobedience is less stressful and easier to enact than all of that tweeting and letter writing. In the meantime, I'm off to walk up a mountain where the only parliament is of the rooks and the most important distance is the one between me and my darker thoughts.

Poly-mathematics and the need to let go

Every so often a friend or fellow blogger will ask if I still paint. The honest answer is that I don't, though I will usually fudge it by saying something like *I occasionally draw,* or *only for fun.* In many ways, this isn't a total deception: I take an interest in images; I love art shops; I think in a visual way... In my mind, I could pick up my brushes tomorrow.

But it wouldn't work.

Painting seriously takes practice and dedication—as does running, or chess, or physics... Occasionally, people refer to me as a polymath (one blogger did so yesterday), but in truth, I mostly focus on one thing at a time. If I want to lose weight it will obsess me till I'm thinner; if work is busy I tend not to write for pleasure; when I learned to play the saxophone, it consumed me for two years—in retrospect, a bad idea.

Why?

Because I'll never be any good at jazz.

Sure, I can bash out a tune and fake the odd riff, but deep down I'm not a musician—and no amount of practice will change that. What's more, it's an all too easy distraction from those projects that in my heart I know are more important. Writers are notorious for finding excuses to delay; sometimes we need simply to focus and type—in my case, with the noise turned down.

Not that I shall sell my saxophone. For I've learned to stop playing when it matters and to see that as something gained rather than lost. The same is true of painting: to begin again wouldn't be right, but that doesn't mean all interest has gone. My love of the outdoors is similarly slimmed-down: I still kayak and cycle and climb mountains, but in a less obsessive way.

This is good, I think.

For there is pleasure in learning and letting go.

Five years ago I taught myself basic French, but let's be honest, I'm never going to be fluent. Mountains and wild places have been a joy of my life—in some ways they saved it—but to continue quite so full-on, might well end it prematurely. I could make an equivalent point about poetry or fiction: I wrote them for my degree and learned a great deal, but they are not my genre. Though interestingly, I write often in a 'fictive form', constructing my blogs and essays not dissimilarly to short stories. I obsess too over words, in the way of a poet.

And this illustrates how in letting go, we don't lose all that we've gained.

It's four decades since I studied economics, and yet in drafting this piece I originally wrote a line in a paragraph above: '...*the law of diminishing returns sates that once optimal capacity is reached, further growth requires disproportionate resources...*' Thanks for that are due to my teacher, Mr Johnson; I owe much the same debt to Ms Davies who taught me to draw.

But for all it's good to have a reservoir of knowledge, the fact I chose to reposition the sentence is due to an experienced eye, which saw that it added more elsewhere. That judgement—and intensity of focus—comes only with practice, and were I more rusty, I'd probably have missed it. This is the dilemma we face in pursuing our passions: how to balance the breadth and depth of our skills and understanding.

Though actually, that's not quite correct, because a true dilemma is a choice between two outcomes, both of which are bad. There is no word for its opposite, so it seems to me that in our choosing one over the other we are more in the realm of preference. Both are equally good, and can feed off each other, as do music and dance, science and nature... or, for that matter, writing and painting.

Dogs know what to say

'Dogs are good when you're going through tough times—they just know what to say.' Those words came from a text my friend sent me after they learned we'd had sad news. For the last fortnight, Jane has been nursing her mum, our lives temporarily upended—suspended even—as we come to terms with the limits of life.

It seems (at least in our case) that we settle quickly into roles laid down over millennia: the women caring, the men keeping going; each clutching to some semblance of normality. This week I have been in Pembrokeshire, writing and working—they merge into one, like sky and sea. Time alone feels like an indulgence, and yet there's pragmatism in it too; life goes on, jobs to be done...

Yesterday I walked with Oscar to the high cliffs at St David's Head. There were many other pilgrims, stopping for photographs at what's a highlight of the coastal path. People have been coming here for generations, seeking solace and salvation at this ending of the road. Near the car park, archaeologists are excavating a mediaeval chapel; one hundred graves are aligned east to west in the path of the sun.

It doesn't take us long to reach the cove at Porthmelgan, but already, I sense Oscar knows things are not right. He walks close to my knees, not from any shortening of the leash but because he's done so all week; his eyes check me every few yards. Where is his pack, why are we not together on the beach? When we reach the headland he settles by my side, nose on my shoulder, snuffling in a soft steady rhythm.

Out at sea, there are gannets patrolling the flows and avenues of the tide, gliding effortlessly over what to them is its limpid surface. On the cliffs, there's a band of orange lichen that marks the limits of the salt spray, a hundred feet above the water. The rocks it washes are a mixture of granite and sediment that's half a billion years old.

In places like this, it's natural to see our lives in perspective. We talk of being grains of sand, stars in the heavens... insignificant moments in a landscape of space and time that's beyond our knowing. And yet we come here to make connections too. For we are as much a part of this place as it is of us—like the countless trillions of quarks and atoms and cells which make up our collective whole. Had we the capacity, we could trace our roots to the genesis that brought all this into being and will ultimately bring it to an end.

The philosopher John Gray says we humans are straw dogs, fated to be forgotten and deluded by our sense of difference as a species. His reasoning—and his writing—is compelling and persuasive for those of us without faith. And yet, for all its deductive potency, it somehow 'feels' wrong, because we don't sense or act as if our lives are insignificant, whatever the lack of a greater scheme.

The problem with metaphors like 'grains of sand' and 'stars in the heavens' is that they are too static and temporally removed; they take no account of our churning of the waters; the disturbance in the sediment created by the waves and wakes of our lives. Our actions may not make much impression on the granite of time, but there's value in the here and now, in the love and care and difference we make to our fractions of the universe, which are just as essential and eternal as any other.

Across the ridge to the north is Coetan Arthur, the capstone remains of a neolithic burial chamber. It seems our forefathers' found significance here too and, walking towards it, I find myself wondering if it also was aligned to the sun. Jane loves this sense of history, the thought that people before us were thinking and acting just as we do. She would like to be here I'm sure, but wouldn't have it otherwise for now.

As I sat with Oscar looking back on the path we'd taken, I wondered what he saw and was thinking. His ribs were pressing on my back, and I remembered that message from my friend—that dogs know just what to say. That's a non-sequitur of sorts because, of course, we know they can't speak. Perhaps that's the point.

Turning tide

It's seldom that I publish blogs of what are effectively notes from a journey—this post was an exception to the rule, which perhaps shows possibilities of the form.

Thursday, 8.30 am, Dale, Pembrokeshire.

What was it I wrote yesterday, *'when it's wet, go to the caff.'*

Not an option today—it's coming over in sheets.

We walk across the mouth of River Gann, the mudflats teaming with gulls and waders; a golden eye and a cormorant in the pools to our left. A solitary fisherman is digging for bait in the silt, his Jack Russell scampering across the flats towards us; it stops, yaps, and an egret rises from the marsh. The Gann is one of the premier bird watching locations in Pembrokeshire, in weather like today all manner of species seek refuge in its sheltered waters.

The tide is lapping the stepping stones, a little higher than I'd hoped. No problems for now, but we'll need to hurry to Sandy Haven, where a tributary stream is only passable at low water. We press on, trying to ignore the sting of the rain.

The Daugleddau estuary is one of the deepest natural harbours in the world. For decades the refineries and storage plants brought prosperity to Milford Haven and Pembroke Dock. Many of the facilities have closed, but not all, and this is still an important port for oil and gas supplies.

As we walked, I thought of the contrast with the River Tyne, where my father and grandfather worked at Swan Hunters. Only vaguely can I remember the shipyards at anywhere near capacity, or even the passage of boats on the river, or the dry docks where they came for repair. I do remember the building of the Esso Northumbria, the largest oil tanker in the world at the time, and the pride in the town when she was launched.

By the time we reach Sandy Haven the stepping stones are under water that is getting deeper by the minute. We can either wade across or make a five mile diversion on dull roads in rain that will make us just as wet. I take off my boots and start over, using my pole to steady me against the flow. Half way across I hesitate and assess the situation. My friend presses on and I follow; act now or be damned. We laugh at the far bank, pleased with our decisiveness—by the time our socks are back on our feet the tide has risen further and our chosen route no longer an option.

Reaching the oil terminals, I'm surprised at the lack of ships and empty docking platforms. Perhaps the weather was a factor, for it was near here that the Sea Empress ran aground in 1994, spewing oil across most of Pembrokeshire Coast. Often the tankers wait in St Brides Bay for the storms to subside before entering the harbour.

I'm conscious that in most landscapes I dislike the intrusion of technology—I've ranted often about the wind-farms that so despoil the Cambrian Mountains. But this place has long given itself over to industry and the lower estuary has been used by shipping for five thousand years. It's still its defining feature: there are marinas at every inlet; the ferry leaves for Ireland twice a day; pilots chug between the many active jetties. These are all well and good, but it's the big ships that give it most character, and today the waters looked lonely without them.

Rounding the headland at Milford, I notice a new vessel docked on a pontoon. It's neither a tanker nor a container ship, more a combination of the two; four silver pipes connect it to the land, where a spaghetti of tubes enters a futuristic building in front of grey storage domes. This is the new liquid gas plant, a project that has regenerated the disused refinery. It looks more hopeful than I'd expected.

We reach the marina, the rain streaming down the hill which bounds the harbour. Milford feels like a town teetering on the edge; down but not quite out. Sixteen years ago the Tall Ships race came here; there were plans for a major regeneration, the quayside was tarted up and units built for cafes and chandleries. It hasn't quite worked. I'd bet a lot of money that only a handful of the yachts are owned by locals.

We take shelter in Tesco, a pool of water gathering around our feet. The tills are busy and it's a far cry from the desperate stores I've seen in Newport or the South Wales Valleys. I hope it stays that way. I hope the new investment works better than the fancy plan for tourism that was always a long shot.

But I'm not optimistic.

For amongst the Christmas tinsel, there are tell-tale signs of decay: the locked spirits cabinet, the drug abuse posters, the small display of fresh vegetables—and the lengthening queue for the lottery.

Blood nosed beetle

Beetles are extraordinary creatures. They are among our most beautiful insects, they play a vital role in our ecosystem; many have astonishing life-cycles. And yet of 4000 species in the UK, I could put a name to around a dozen, which is almost certainly more than most people.

We ought to know more about beetles.

Last Friday as I walked to St David's Head we came across the chap in the photo above. He was crossing the coast path near to Porth Melgan, and looked vulnerable to being preyed on by birds so I gave him a helping hand. He's a bloody nosed beetle, one of the commoner species in Pembrokeshire, and October is evidently late for him to be out and about.

Quite why I've decided this beetle is a 'he', I can't say, for in truth I've no idea of its gender. Identification is tough enough; sexing them damn near impossible. There isn't a fully comprehensive UK field guide, though to be fair, a huge number of those 4000 species will be LBJs (Little Brown Jobs). I generally use Michael Chinery's *Pocket Guide to Insects* or even the (more truly pocketable) Collins Gem series. Other than that, I take a photo and try my luck on Google or one of the many insect forums.

But in a way, identification barely matters.

This particular one crawled over my hand, each step a soft and delicate placement, tickling my palm—his exoskeleton iridescent in the light. I thought he was gorgeous, and if I were forty years younger I'd have popped him in a matchbox as a pet! Bloody nosed beetles are named for their habit of discharging a red fluid when threatened—this foul-smelling liquid deters predators. Thankfully he didn't spew up on my hand and I like to think that he sensed I meant him no harm.

I laid him down in some tall grass by a drystone wall. He'll not survive the winter, but his larvae will, and next year there'll be more of these fascinating creatures under our feet—if ever we care to look.

The last light of summer

Beneath me as I write is the sweep of the sea on the western tip of Wales. I'm sitting in the van, my whippet curled beside me, the sky paling to the thinner evening light. It's been a bright day; the beach was busy with trippers, the campsites fuller than usual. But soon, the sun will arc to the horizon, and the last light of summer will be gone.

My grandfather used to insist that autumn proper began with the equinox—I have his sundial still in my garden. At junior school, we marked the turning of the season with a harvest festival later in September. And I suppose, horologically at least, British Summer Time will be with us till October.

But for me, the rituals that mark the transition are more secular and less scientific. The other week I put away the garden furniture and somehow knew it wouldn't come out again. Then there's the buying of school uniform, the ordering of an academic wall chart, the sense that September, not January, is when the year should begin.

This summer has passed too quickly.

My grandfather would point out that such a notion is nonsense; that the world turns at a constant speed regardless of our desires. Yet, when I saw small copper butterflies on the coast path today, it seemed only weeks since the first brood in spring. And, according to a birder I met, the linnets are departing, and an osprey has arrived on the Daugleddau.

Jane says she likes the autumn and, in theory, I do too: the prospect of crisp leaves under steel skies, of sloes and hips and haws, of turnip lanterns and penny for the guy... In Northumberland, where I grew up, the season is typically dry and cold—crisp, we'd call it. Here, it brings September swells, a greyer light, if warmer sea, and for me, an intangible sense of days that can never come again.

Of course, the seasons are not as rigid as our calendars or meteorologists would have them. Nor would nature regard autumn as either beginning or end. The last light of summer is no more than a poetic metaphor, resonant to a darkening sky and the lamentations of a writer no longer in the flush of his youth.

My friend, the author Jim Perrin, described the west as the landscape of loss; as where the light dies. He was drawn to the Atlantic coast in unspeakable grief at the deaths of his son and wife. As a child, my school overlooked an eastern sea; a pink sky in the morning was a fisherman's warning, we were told. Here, all is reversed.

So as I sit and watch the clouds redden over Ramsey, I'm mindful that fair weather will follow. That the troubles of this year, its fears and fall-outs, its sunshine and showers… as they say, this too will pass. I hope so, and not before long.

For in truth, I have loathed the lockdown, and all that came with it: the shrinking of our lives, the sub-surface tensions, the fibs we tell each other and ourselves to hold it all in check. If ever a summer was craved, it was this one, and yet at times, I would gladly have slept through it all. That's somewhat dark, but it's also truth to power of how I've felt and in so being, a little lighter to bear.

Tomorrow my youngest son returns to school. The world will no doubt spin as always, and the geese and fieldfares will follow it in their turn. I have builders at my house, a new study to construct. Somewhere, if I can find them, a book or two to write.

In Welsh, the word *cynheaf* means both autumn and harvest. That we reap what we sow has been an aphoristic ear-worm to my year. I worry that our pickings will be thin, that in focusing our minds, we've narrowed our perspectives; in our terror of the dark, we've ironically dimmed the light.

It's cold now. The sea is nearing and the glow from the laptop is all that remains. I should move on. My little whippet is restless, unnerved by our evening sojourn in the van. He too misses the warmth of the sun.

Interlude:
The blog as essay

The essayist Chris Arthur, includes an afterward to his virtuoso collection, *Hummingbirds Between the Pages*, titled, 'Thirty Six Ways of Looking at an Essay'. It takes the form of short epithets that offer a multitude of lenses on the possibilities of the form. My favourite describes the essay as 'a net for catching butterfly moments as they fly past'. Another asserts that the essay is as far removed from a scholarly article as a sonnet from a butcher's cleaver.

In corresponding with Arthur on his writing we briefly discussed the relationship of blogs to the essay. Are they essentially the same, or should we consider blogging to be a form of its own? Will the posts of today ever be reprinted in the way that the musings of Hazlitt or Twain are now? Or is blogging doomed to be ephemeral, ultimately transient writing, lasting only as long as the service providers allow and our subscriptions maintain?

In part, these questions are confused by the different and yet overlapping meanings of the terms. Writing the paragraph above, I refer to blogs as both a form and format, alternating between the two with ease of commonplace usage. My doing so reminds me of how, years ago, I worked in consumer marketing and the talk at that time was of controlling the 'content and channel' to an audience: Disney Corporation was regarded as the master.

Today, when someone speaks of a blog—or in my case, says they write one—we typically think of a simplified website, owned and curated by its author, usually self-published, and available to anyone who searches or stumbles upon it. This is the domain of WordPress and Blogger, it's where I started out and where millions of us continue to plough our furrows.

But it's only one perspective.

Commercial websites will often include a section labelled 'Blog' and we instinctively know what we'll find there is something slightly different. Frankly, we know there's a good chance it'll be tired and forgotten, but if not, it will host a range of topical articles covering news and information of relevance to the site's visitors. Look up almost any copy writing agency and you'll see them touting services to provide companies with a *regular flow of engaging content*... I should know; I write these for my clients all the time.

The philosopher Ludwig Wittgenstein argued that some terms were not strictly definable; rather, our understanding was more one of a familial resemblance: games and sports, are the often quoted examples. Might the term blog qualify too?

From home bloggers to copywriters to agitators, such as Dominic Cummings writing for political change (and in a more traditional blog format than you might imagine), what we think of as a blog is something distinct and yet fluid, recognised in part by what it isn't, as much as what it is. Blogs are not magazines, or books, or academic journals, or private diaries, or....

Essays?

Well, that would depend on what it is we write—and to some extent on how it's read.

The posts in this volume have, I hope, it's fair to say, a resemblance to the genre. My first book, *Counting Steps*, punctuates its longer-form essays with shorter pieces that were initially published on *Views from the Bike Shed*. On my shelves are collections of writings that include Twain, Orwell, Borrow, Grayling, Hitchens, Turgenev, Montaigne... centuries of reflections, much of which could comfortably be published as a blog post today.

But while it's clear there is some familial similarity, I'm not sure there's much to be gained in searching for a pure bloodline. Not least, we might question why the style of blog post which interests me should be considered the pedigree genre? The online diaries of the millions of bloggers who've never considered themselves to be writers in any serious sense, have just as much claim to that epithet—arguably more. That not all blogs are essays is as plain as a pikestaff and about as unbending by way of ultimate conclusion.

Nonetheless—and laden with these caveats—I'm going to assert that the blog post has at least some claim to be a sibling of the essay.

Siblings of course are never identical—even congenital twins will differ by nature. Almost always, blogs are written in the first person; and typically they are topical, at least in the sense that they offer fresh thoughts. I write every post—from notion to conclusion—in pretty much one sitting, and though it might stretch to a few days on occasions, a piece that's gestated for months, has surely weakened its status as a weblog.

It may be obvious, but the pedant in me demands that blog posts need to be original works, written for the web—we wouldn't consider Martin Luther King's Letter from Birmingham Jail to qualify, no matter how often it was retrospectively posted. This is why poetry blogs seldom work well—they may use the familial format but their content is at best that of second cousin twice removed.

Perhaps the one definitive thing we can say about blogs, as opposed to the essay, is that they are written to be read online. And that this has an impact which is more significant than it might first seem.

Many years ago—early in my blogging career—I attended a residential writing course on which we were asked to share an example of our work. To save time, I printed off a post and passed copies round the class, rather proud of the words I'd written. The tutor, however, seemed more concerned in critiquing its format. 'Oh, a blog post, how interesting,' he said. 'Now, let's look at the title—what's that telling us?... and the use of a picture too...'

I recall interjecting and saying it was the writing which mattered; that the screen grab was merely a quick way of making a copy of the words.

But he carried on regardless.

At the time, I was irritated by his determination to focus on what seemed to me an irrelevance. Looking back now, I realise he was right. For though it's certainly possible to separate the content from the form—this book is proof of that—as bloggers we need to recognise that the way—and where—we present our work to others, changes how it will be read.

We know, for example, that the way people read on screens is very different to the way they interact with books and magazines. The device we read on makes a difference too. Even something as simple as scrolling changes the dynamic from that of turning a page. As writers we might wish to pretend these differences don't matter, they do.

For a start, attention span is shorter online: beyond 1,000 words and you'll struggle to hold interest; to publish a 5,000 word article on a website is as good as inviting it to be printed off. There are occasional longer reads, but it's significant that they're usually flagged as such, much like they are in the weekend newspapers and supplements.

I could go on, but all we'd find is yet more resemblance and disparity—a repetition of theme and variation, such that the sequencing of any blog's DNA returns one part this, five parts that, two of something else...

Perhaps the most we can say is that blogs are a sort of mongrel form. Which, in the way of serendipitous thoughts, brings to mind an analogy with domestic dogs, all of which are one species descended from wolves (*Canis lupus familiaris*) but which, over the centuries, have been classified into so-called breeds that we recognise as distinct and yet the same.

Who cares if blogs are pure-bred or not? Certainly not me.

I'm no doubt biased, but what I see in blogging is more people than ever putting words to the page, with their content and channels being adapted to their purposes as surely as are shopping lists and manuscripts.

Somewhere in the 570 million blogs that are reportedly online, there is writing of real worth and impact (if you doubt the latter, read something of the recent history of Eastern Europe to see how blogs can galvanise people and politics). These bloggers—or at least some of them—are the descendants of the country diarists, the columnists, the angry letter writers, the pamphleteers... of Francis Kilvert and Daniel Defoe and indeed Chris Arthur.

We'd need more than thirty-six ways to view that miscellany; a sort of spider's eye view perhaps... but then that's an essay (or a post) in itself.

Full circle

Somewhere in our album of family photographs is a picture of my father being held aloft as a baby. He must only be a few months old and presumably the arm holding him skyward is that of my grandfather. Turn a few pages and you'd find an almost identical picture of my elder brother in the same pose, his christening shawl bright against a Northumbrian sky. I've no memory of it being taken because I wasn't yet born, but I do distinctly recall my dad referring often to the images, and musing, in philosophic tone, how history repeats itself in families.

It's strange the incidents and words we remember. My father must have spoken of a thousand other events, sharing his past life (as we all do with our children) through recollections that would invariably shape mine, or at least my outlook on it. The reason some stick and others are lost is more, I suspect, a matter of chance and circumstance (*was I hungry or distracted as he spoke*) than any logic or weighing of import. Often, as in this case, it is particular images or phrases that trigger our recall. And with each repetition, what we actually remember is our previous recollections... such that over time our memories become as fixed and falsely representative as snapshots in an album.

Quite why I was drawn to compose this introduction is in equal parts obvious and obscure. As will become clear, I've recently been revisiting my past by proxy, returning to rock climbing after a gap of nearly thirty years. I'd planned to open by describing how as a young man I was so determined to achieve and experience as much as I could; how even in my twenties there was a certain rage against the dying of the light—a feeling that time was limited and I a had duty to make the most of it; carpe diem, gather ye rosebuds... make hay while the sun shines...

I feel much of this urgency still, though as I grow older I find that I'm less concerned with pressing on than with doubling back. Perhaps at some level I'm afraid the memories I hold most dear will otherwise fade or falsify, and hope that by re-experiencing them I might somehow remaster their clarity. There could be truth in that I guess... But returning to why I wrote the introduction, I sense my recent reliving of past passions is less about history repeating itself than a desire to come full circle.

Earlier this month I went with my eldest son to Raven Crag in Borrowdale. We climbed a route called Corvus that's about as old school as it gets. Tied together for seven pitches we ascended a line I'd last followed, according to the notes in my guide book, thirty-three years previously. The small blue volume has a grainy photograph depicting an exposed hand traverse that's the crux of the climb and an iconic image of mountaineering from a bygone era. What it doesn't show is the big ledge below and out of shot—the only part of the route I remembered correctly.

The following day we visited Langdale to climb Middlefell Buttress—ironically on a cliff also called Raven Crag. This time my old guidebook had no notes and although I distinctly recalled the situation and indeed my former ascent, I could not for the life of me—at least with any certainty—remember my partner. We joked about whether I'd climbed it with his mum or my first wife years before; 'awkward' he laughed. True—but in that shared humour we forged a moment that will live with us both and likely be more genuine than any memories of the holds or stances or sequence we followed.

I've long felt that the best and most satisfying journeys start and finish, if not always from home, at least from the place we began. In my father's case, his memories were invariably sentimental though. in fairness, often funny too. What struck me at the time, and to some extent troubles me still, is how at odds they were with the depression and self-loathing that so coloured his adulthood. It was as if by seeking to forge a supposedly better future he'd severed all connections with the few happy years of his life.

Memories. of course, are not located in a physical place or moment in time, rather we carry them with us as bounty or burdens depending on our state of mind. I know that I will never again climb with the skill and strength I once possessed. I know too that my son must find his own routes and not live in the shadow of mine. Perhaps that's why I took no photographs of us roped together; because I don't want him to be tied to my past just as I don't believe that history must repeat itself in families. And yet, conversely, might sharing and showing him where I came from be just enough for our circles to overlap?

Ripples on the sand

The beach this evening was all silhouettes; the tide ebbing as a westering sun cast shadows on the pools and rippled sand. A young couple walked hand in hand, paddling barefoot in the shallows. Oscar was having none of that, running instead over the silver streams that mirage the two-mile stretch to Rickets Head.

I've walked this way a hundred times. When our older boys were small, we'd come here day after day, them never tiring of the want to splash and dig. Back then it sometimes felt too open, too windswept—and too much a place where movement was needed, rather than the standing around and building of castles and dams that comes with little ones in wellies.

It's different now. Oscar wants nothing other than his ball: throw and return; throw and return... such grace in the way he runs, so swift he outpaces my fling. Whippets, I read the other day, are the fastest accelerating dogs. I can believe it, as he sets off for the umpteenth time, his chase instinct stronger than any distracting scent or passing pooch.

My youngest son—who's now in his teens—was obsessed with mechanical contraptions as a child. Try as I might, he took no interest in landscape or nature. Even camping, which he liked, was all about process not place; no sooner had we pitched the tent than he'd snuggle down and watch videos on the iPad—preferably of trains. The cottage beach, as he's always called it, was, and still is, one of his few exceptions to the rule.

Which is pleasing, as we're relocating here full time, and walks like this will be part of the daily ebb and flow. To live within minutes of such a fabulous spot is a joy and privilege—for it to also be your favourite, must double the pleasure. Or in my case, triple it, for this stretch of sand and pebbles is redolent of memories I treasure; of times that will never come again.

Or at least, not quite.

This evening, as I walked back to the car there was a family near the breakwater which borders the road. Two toddlers in oversize anoraks and blue welly boots stomped in the puddles—they built piles of pebbles and ran in circles together as their mum and dad (mid-thirties I'd guess) watched with collars turned up.

'I must have a hundred photos of mine doing the same,' I said. 'In this very spot too'.

'So it's not just us,' they replied, smiling.

We got to talking about parenting boys that are close in age, the companionship they have, the hardship they bring—and the joys too... I spoke of the times we'd spent on this beach, the pattern of our days determined by the tides...

By now their boys were sitting in the water making sand pies.. 'Spare clothes in the car,' we said in unison—me as a question, her as a statement.

I laughed.

'We never planned to have two so close,' she said.

'Neither did we,' I replied. 'Our first was conceived with IVF, the second a complete surprise...' And from the look on her face I knew what she'd say next.

'We were the same!'

Her husband chipped in, 'We were told we'd not have children without treatment—or at least it was very unlikely. Then before we knew it we had two...'

'Buy one, get one free,' I quipped, explaining that in our day there was no NHS funded fertility service.

Oscar began scratching at my pockets for his ball. 'It was nice to meet you,' they said, as I put him on the lead.

'You've taken me back,' I replied, shaking my head in disbelief...

By now, the sun was almost to the sea, the air chilling in the way that spring evenings do. I climbed the bank of stones and wondered how imperceptibly slower my movements will become each year. At the top I paused; there were new silhouettes on the sand—night fishermen, casting lines from the shore.

The tide here is a long time turning.

Gather ye rosebuds while ye may

Gather ye rosebuds while ye may,
Old time is still a flying;
And this same flower that smiles today,
Tomorrow will be dying
Robert Herrick

There's a famous scene in the film *Dead Poet's Society* in which the inspirational John Keating (played by Robin Williams) tells his pupils to look closely at the photographs of old boys on the walls. His instruction follows a reading of the poem above, lamenting the brevity of life, and urging us to seize the day. Look at those faces, says Keating, they're like you... the same haircuts, same hormones... full of hope...

Yesterday, I dug out my own alumni picture: the sixth form class of '79 at Whitley Bay High School. I'm on the back row, fourth from the left, arms folded and tie askew. Of the 120 or so faces I could perhaps name 30 and no doubt more if prompted. My girlfriend, and later wife, is to the right of the middle row; my best man (twice now) has his face obscured.

Other than Rebecca and Ken, I have no contact with any of the others. I learned yesterday that there is to be a reunion in September; it will be 49 years since we started high school together. Some of those pictured were my friends in primary too; one was my desk mate on the very first day. How strange that we might meet again?

Here in Wales, Jane and her family have closer connections to the community; it helps perhaps that her father was a headmaster. But more than that, by staying relatively local, the interweaving of lives is more traceable; the network of paths less easily lost. Thirty years ago, I moved 300 miles south and west, severing the threads, if not quite the ties to my past.

In that experience, I won't be alone. At least half of those facing the camera went on to university; few will have returned to the town we grew up in. Opportunities and progress are more dispersed than in the time of our parents, and of theirs before them… In a sense, all our histories are diasporas of a sort.

And it's this thought which fascinates me most about the photograph.

If I think of the hopes and talents that are captured in its pixels, the possibilities are infinite. What roads have we all travelled—what roots are laid down? Did our futures play out as predicted by our teachers—or as we ourselves had planned? Somehow I doubt it. And if we were to stand together again today, how many of us would there be—surely some will have been lost?

But none of this is maudlin. For life is good, and we cannot undo the choices we make, or for that matter our fates. Did we go on to have extraordinary lives? In many respects—and certainly, in historical terms—we will all of us have lived remarkably. That we are now approaching our sixties is itself an astonishing thought. So too, how swiftly we've travelled, how fragile the footprints we leave.

I was thinking all this as we walked in the woodland near our home yesterday evening. Jane asked if I was with her at all; her forbearance of my inner world as patient as ever. On the rise of the hill, we sat listening to birdsong, and all around us were countless seeds floating in the air. Some were falling nearby, others being carried on the breeze… what plants will they sow I wondered; where and when will they flower?

And what of my sons; two of them older now than I was in the picture? As parents, we might wish for our offspring to spread like tendrils, but there's a reason why seeds disperse in wind or water. Few trees grow tall in the shadow of others; it's their scattering afar that allows them to flourish. They must do so also when the time is right.

Herrick's poem is often twinned with Shakespeare's warning that 'Rough winds do shake the darling buds of May / And summers lease hath all too short a date…' In the famous film scene, Keating tells his pupils not to wait for chance or circumstance. The old boys in the pictures, he says, are now fertilising daffodils—we are all of us, 'food for worms'.

That's true, but not quite yet.

The faces of my classmates were full of promise. I hope our reunion is as much a celebration of life still to live, as that which has passed. After all, there's much to be said for an Indian summer.

Soar y Mynydd

The Soar-y-Mynydd chapel is often cited as the most remote in Wales. I'm not sure how that calculation is made, but it's certainly one of the most beautiful and makes for a fine pilgrimage when walking or cycling in the *Green Desert of Wales*—a Victorian description of the Cambrian Mountains which, in many ways, remains appropriate.

In describing Soar-y-Mynydd as beautiful, I'm defying convention: austere, would be equally apt; forbidding, not out of place. But then beauty comes in different forms. My neighbour is a stonemason who's indifferent to ornate carving but delights in the millimetre accuracy of cathedral pillars. He would like Soar-y-Mynydd, not for its stonework, but its simplicity: the symmetrical arrangement of the boxed pews, the lack of adornment, the sparse use of colour.

I like the windows too: tall with Gothic points inside a rounded arch, no stained glass. They remind me of my junior school, which is perhaps not surprising because the chapel was conjoined to one until it closed in the 1940s. To picture the community then is to imagine a lost world. Last weekend, three cars were parked on the drive; the information board says that in its heyday, sixty horses were regularly tethered on Sundays!

The landscape has transformed too.

Down the hill is the Llyn Brianne reservoir, built in the Seventies to provide water for South Wales, it consumed the upper Tywi to near its meeting with the Doethie. Interestingly, I can't find a reference to the name of the valley before it was flooded (*the river above it is the Camddwr, but perhaps it was just known as Tywi*). An excellent local website says the reservoir is actually a misspelling of a minor tributary, the Nant y Bryniau (literally, the stream in the hills).

Above the waterline are the ubiquitous conifer forests that cover too much of the Cambrian Mountains. To be fair, the planting began long before the dam was constructed, and of all the mid Wales reservoirs

Llyn Brianne seems to blend more sensitively, even delightfully, into the hills. We walked a five-mile section last Sunday and saw redstarts, dragonflies, a tortoiseshell butterfly and a soaring buzzard—no kites at the dam, but they were there at the RSPB reserve below.

I first came to Llyn Brianne a month after moving to Wales, mistaking the mountain road as a potential easy option on a cycle tour. In the twenty years since I must have returned at least once each year, often more frequently. Reflecting last weekend, I realised it's become central to my image and understanding of this part of Wales. And it's full of good memories—of nights in the Dolgoch hostel, of backpacking with my boys, cycling the Tregaron road; of my friends, kayaking the overspill on the dam (an activity now banned).

And of Soar-y-Mynydd too.

I have no religious faith, but if I did, I think I'd be 'chapel' not 'church'. So it's good to know the pews are still used—and sometimes even filled. For evidently Soar-y-Mynydd has become an oasis in the desert—parishioners travel miles to attend its services and preachers consider it a great honour to be invited. A friend told me they are all firebrands, bible-bashers of the old school. I like to think of them ranting to the congregation as the rain hammers the windows and the Avon Camwddwr runs brackish and inextricably towards the dam.

Dusk and dust

Above the town of Blaenavon at the head of the Afon Llwyd valley is a disused drift mine on the flank of Coity Mountain. The road which once serviced it remains a conspicuous contour on the hillside—though not in the way of a scar, for it has blended well into the moorland, offering the prospect of a gentle if longish climb to the now dilapidated works.

I went there the other week, my third visit in as many months. It's a melancholy place, occupying those seductive edges of past and present, industry and nature, that tempt us to attribute it with meaning, when in fact, there is only what is there.

It's beautiful nonetheless. The skeleton of the old shed silhouettes against the sky, rusted beams tone with the autumn bracken and violet horizon of the Black Mountains to the north. Even the graffiti seems apposite—adding a kingfisher flash to an otherwise limited palette.

When I showed some photos to a friend, he asked me, 'Have you ever seen *Hinterland*?' referring to the noir detective series that's filmed in Mid Wales. It's set in a landscape that evokes something of a cross between the Old Testament and frontier homesteads. The original Welsh language version was titled Y Gwyll, which means 'the dusk'— that time between twilight and darkness; the opposite of dawn.

I had to look the translation up, and at first misread it, thinking— until checking a few days later—that 'gwyll' meant 'dust'. How pertinent, for writerly purposes, that link would have been: nature reclaiming its own; steel leaching rust to the earth, the walls of the pithead crumbling... and the coal in the lungs of the miners...

You see, how easy it is to impute meaning.

I guess I could do the same with dusk—weave a narrative about the twilight of mining, reference the Big Pit Museum, the shadows of the men who worked these seams... It turns out that the drift on Coity

Mountain—known as Blaentillery—was actually the last in the area to close, opening in the Sixties and struggling on till early this century.

I often wonder about the prospects for the South Wales Valleys. Ultimately, these are communities whose original purpose has gone. Years ago they would have decayed like the mine; today we won't, can't, bring ourselves to allow that to happen. And so they struggle on too, occupying an indeterminate ground, lacking the skills and infrastructure to remodel their future, yet too rent by the past for a transition to tourism.

And hence the melancholy—which it's all too easy for outsiders like me to romanticise when that gift (if that's the right word) is hardly mine to bestow. If there's any meaning in place it lies not in the landscape *in and of itself*, but in our relationships to it. Those who lived and worked here would no doubt have a different—and truer— perspective than my three visits in as many months can hope to conjure.

But that's as it should be. For whenever I walk the tops of these hills I sense that despite knowing them for half my life, their valleys will always be something apart. I look down to the ribbon rows of houses not so much with sadness, as curiosity—even a little envy.

And ironically, I remember that the reason I first came here, was they reminded me of home.

Dodd Wood—and the paths we follow

Dodd Wood is an unassuming tump on the western flank of Skiddaw in the English Lake District. Alfred Wainright in his guide to the Lakeland Fells deemed it a whelp of its loftier neighbour but was otherwise kind in his assessment of the forestation that's turned a forgettable also-ran into something more distinct. These days it's managed by Forestry England, the bright and breezy rebrand of what for years we'd known as the Forestry Commission.

Not that there was any sparkle in the sky this morning, the rain so persistent that the higher summits were out of the question and even a trip round town would have required a level of cajoling that only another whippet owner would appreciate. But as the clouds lifted and the downpour eased, somewhere in the recesses of my mind sprang a memory of this little hill and its sheltered paths.

Dodd Wood's network of trails is approached by the road that hugs the shores of Bassenthwaite Lake. Forty years ago, fresh from sitting my A-levels, I'd stayed near here for what turned out to be one of those coming of age holidays where the girls fall out and the boys are pulled twixt and tween in a way that lays bare the naïveties of youth. On our first night, the group split into those who'd expected single-sex sleeping and others keen to take advantage of the opposite.

And so it was that the next day my girlfriend and I set off up this little hill, her crying like this morning's downpour because her friend now hated her—and me as well because she'd said as much... It was a lesson for her in the fragility of friendship, and for me in the rectitude and reproach that's a scratch from the surface of those whose greatest fear is themselves.

And I remember thinking, as we climbed under the clouds of the day, that you can never truly know anyone else...

More than forty years later my view on that point hasn't changed, and I still look for solace in remote and wild places. Except that description isn't quite complete, for the indifference of the landscape is as much an affirmation as consolation. Mountains—even small ones like today's climb—are a means of connecting to the secular truth that no matter our closeness to others—however in step they may seem—we walk our paths alone.

The route to the top of Dodd Wood is a three-mile circuit, following the green arrows of Forestry England's new designated trails. Along the way, they've strategically felled sections to reveal views of Derwentwater and the Newlands Valley. As we stopped for a breather, I reeled off the peaks in my mind: Causey Pike, Barrow, Cat Bells… friends from years long past…

Whatever happened, I wondered, to Julie and Ian, Claire and Karen, the two Johns… Mark and poor Dave, who'd only come with us to climb, yet found himself tangled in the knots and nooses of a teenage squabble?

The summit slopes have been cleared to reveal a prospect that was hidden back then…

What roads did they take; where are they now; and do they ever, like me, feel the pull of coming full circle?

None of this is maudlin on my part. I'm joyful to be back. The life paths that led me here could not have been planned but were less steep and rugged than they might have been.

My youngest son strolls with me up the final climb, Jane follows close behind—we're joined by a couple with a cocker spaniel called Jarvis which make us all laugh… the sun shines a ladder through the clouds.

My girlfriend came with me on more and bigger hills than Little Dodd—we married in our early twenties and, though we parted five years later, I don't regret the routes we took. I hope she feels the same. For we can't undo our past, and to imagine as much is to deny that it leads to where we are now. The choices and judgements we make—for ourselves and of others—are one-way junctions; there's no going back—we can only come through.

The green arrows guide us to a narrower path. Our whippet is unsure of the bracken but follows me regardless. I've no recollection of the way, which momentarily troubles me, until I realise how ridiculous that notion is—it's autumn not summer, the trees are new growth—it's been forty years for goodness sake!

As we near the car park the trail turns towards Bassenthwaite's shore. Across the lake is the mountain known as Barf; there's a white painted stone on its screes that locals call the Bishop—I've known that for forty years too and yet never ventured that way.

Perhaps, I should see where it leads…

The business of writing

Last week my business insurance was due for renewal. It was time for a review so I rang my provider to discuss the options. After completing the usual security questions, the customer services agent asked, 'Can I confirm your nature of business Mr Charlton—what is it, exactly, that you do?'

The simple answer to this question would be 'I'm a writer.' But invariably, when talking to others, I feel the need to explain that I although I write blogs and essays for myself, I also advise on investor communication, draft marketing campaigns, prepare company reports and... it all gets very complex.

So instead, I told the agent that I have a small agency which specialises in copywriting. 'How about PR and Marketing,' he interjected, 'shall I put you down as that?' A few questions later my insurance was renewed and, for the next twelve months at least, I'm a communications director once again!

An amusing incident, though hardly the stuff of a blog post, let alone the first of a potential series on the writing life. But I'll bet the story resonates with many authors who'll read this piece. Why didn't I just say I was a writer? Would my insurer have allowed that job description? And what sort of cover would they have recommended—third party liability, professional indemnity, or just a very thick skin?

I often make a distinction between my commercial work and what I call 'writing for me'. In part, that's because the later doesn't pay the bills—I'll not earn a penny from this post—but I wonder if it also stems from of a sense that writing for companies isn't quite the real thing. As if it's somehow not what proper writers do?

The author Julia Cameron claims that all forms of the craft are equal—that those who draft computer manuals are as entitled to call themselves writers as those who pen poetry. It's the care for our task, she argues, which defines us. And I'd agree—not least because I've spent the last ten minutes redrafting the two sentences above (and this one) to avoid repeating any words.

I've also read this entire piece aloud what must be a dozen times. And when I say aloud—I mean ALOUD, because in my study I'm allowed to do that, and because it makes a difference and is part of my process. By the time you see this, I'll have reviewed it a dozen times more—and I'd do exactly the same if it were a commercial commission.

Some say that being a writer is as much state of mind as practice. I'm sceptical of that—for though I write a great deal 'in my head', it's the committing of pen to paper—or fingers to keys—which is critical to the craft. And it's only through regular practice that we build our confidence, finding a style of our own and not a copy of the Company's or the company we keep. Ultimately, it's that style my clients are paying for, and it's not so different to what's free on my blog.

In recent years I've been lucky enough to teach a little at the University of the West of England. My involvement has largely been to help students transfer their skills in creative genres to more mainstream career opportunities. I've advised the students that regular blogging is one of the best ways to do this, for it involves all the elements of choice and concision and attention to your audience that commercial work demands. It also teaches that perfection isn't necessary for publication—or for that matter success.

Before finishing this post I went for a walk—which is also good practice by the way—and returned to a message from a client. Could I write a report next week: they'll provide the data if I can thread the narrative… make it personal and compelling, they said. Later, another contact called to thank me for drafting some letters. 'I don't know how you do it,' he said, 'the tone is so hard to get right.' 'There's no great secret,' I replied, 'I just write them for myself.'

So perhaps the distinction between writing for me and writing for work isn't so clear cut after all. And perhaps being a communication director is not so different from being an author. Insurance premiums aside, the writing life is first and foremost about writing for life—and the labels we apply are less important than the words we find and the joy we take.

Reclaiming the sofa and our blogs

Oscar, my little one-year-old whippet, has developed a range of techniques to stake his claim on the sofa. Most times it will be gentle pawing, followed by a quick leap to the gap between cushions and leg. Then comes the turning in circles, or perhaps what we call 'long-dog' which involves lying full stretch between the back of the couch and yours... ever so gently nudging us to where he'd like to sit. It's all very genial, and of course, he's warm, comforting and so clearly delighted that, before we know it, we've accommodated his desires without a qualm. Most evenings, he rewards us with some quite disgusting farts!

Of course, we love him, and wouldn't be without his ways... except perhaps for an evening like this, when both Jane and I have tweaked our backs and I'm remembering the times when there was a little more room. And yet, instead of moving him aside, I find myself doing the human equivalent of his nudging techniques—inching into a position that would give me space to balance the laptop and perhaps read some blogs.

As if that were ever going to happen...

And so it is that Jane's watching TV alone, Oscar has two-thirds of the sofa, and I'm back in my study writing this post on the 'big computer'!

Which got me to thinking, how easily we can be persuaded to accommodate those around us. When we do so for someone we love—be it a person or a dog—it's seldom a problem, indeed any caring parent wouldn't wish it otherwise. But when that change is more insidious—when it's impacting who we are and what we wish to be—then we need to call a halt and recover something of ourselves.

By one of those serendipitous twists of fate, I happened this week to read a number of blog posts that spoke of 'reclaiming' their purpose; others expressed misgivings at deleting opinions which, though honestly expressed, might have upset the blog's audience.

The wish to please our readers—and its bedfellow, the desire not to offend—is a time-honoured dilemma for writers of any genre. A good friend of mine claimed the task is so difficult that it's only through fiction that we can speak the truth. I disagree but am under no illusion that sincerity takes courage. Blogs are invariably written in the first person—there's no hiding who it is that's speaking—they can also attract loyal followings, with comments and interaction that sometimes develop into friendships.

The writer Ursula Le Guin disallowed any feedback on her blog, claiming she didn't want to correspond. But then she was a world-famous author, guaranteed a readership, and not in need of the mutuality that characterises the blogging of us lesser mortals. She didn't need advertising or sponsorship either and, to be fair, many bloggers don't either—and yet I've seen legions of them lured by the Sirens of freebies, endorsements and affiliate schemes.

There's nothing inherently wrong with writing a commercial blog, but if we go that route then we must acknowledge that our course and its destination has changed. I'm reminded of when I worked for a regional newspaper company which, under pressure for revenue, changed its mission statement from '*a trusted source of local news*' to '*we deliver an audience to an advertiser*'. Do you see the difference?

I can tell you that the readers did too—and they left in droves.

Because authenticity matters; it matters to us as bloggers and it matters to those who follow what we write. There are obviously occasions when we should be sensitive and cautious—I self-edit all the time—but we must also be true to the feelings and insights and opinions which make our blogs worthwhile. If we expurgate these—removing what I describe as the 'inner story'—then we are left with writing that's but an empty husk. What does it matter that we had cake for tea, went for a walk or read the paper—it's how it tasted, what we saw, and what made us angry—or smile—that gives life and meaning to what we have to say.

I should perhaps add here that there are many blogs I enjoy which seldom engage in these issues. Their *raison d'être* is more a subtle sharing of life's rhythms and progress; the ebbing and flowing of our visible tides. In many ways, these bloggers are inheritors of a long tradition of the country diary. But they too will know if and when they're withholding, and perhaps also the opposite—on those odd occasions, when they deliver a rant that's so out of keeping it's unsettling to read.

I'm conscious that these reflections are somewhat removed. What do they mean for my writing and *Views from the Bike Shed*? Why did the notion of 'reclaiming' strike such a chord? The events of this last year have dominated my own 'inner story' and yet I decided a while ago not to write any more about the pandemic. Looking further back, I was saying to a writing friend this week that I seldom post now in quite the casual way I did years ago.

I don't have an answer to all those questions; sometimes it's enough just to ponder and declare. What I do know, is that I remain determined to write my blog in a way that's true to me and to be jealous of the space this requires. If I've avoided commenting on the pandemic it's been to protect my own wellbeing rather than sidestepping the sensitivities of others; if I post less informally then that's fine, so long as I'm not putting show before substance. In steering my course, I want to avoid the rocks of disapproval, but even more so, the whirlpool of redaction.

I'd like to think this honours my readers too. Relationships are not strengthened by withholding who we are or what we think; indeed, the sign of their worth is the ability to say what we feel—with care of course, but directly nonetheless. If our candour occasionally gives rise to some tension, then that's the grit in the oyster which makes for a pearl. My favourite author of all time is Jean Rhys, a self-obsessed alcoholic, whose attitudes to life are as far removed from mine as whatever's going on in my whippet's head right now. But oh, the honesty and clarity of her work…

Meanwhile, the evening has turned to night and Oscar has retired to his cage. It's five hours since I started this post and the time has passed in an instant. Jane says that often I'm so lost in my thoughts that were it not for the dog, walking together would be little different to her going alone. I tell her that co-presence is a thing and that I'm talking in my head if not out loud—whippets don't understand anyway. Tomorrow (today, now actually) I'll try and strike a better balance, and no doubt I'll fail as usual—but with luck—and much love—I'm sure we'll come together again on the sofa.

Poppies

A little under three weeks ago I sat with my youngest son on the crest of the Col du Ranfolly, the Pointe de Nyon to our left; the ridge of the Roc d'Enfer sparkling in a cobalt sky. We'd ordered burgers and fries from a *buvette* that supplies the skiers who come here for their annual fix of alpine adrenaline. In truth, it's as pre-packaged an experience as the fast-food we were about to tuck into.

I'm not being critical here, just telling the truth as I see it. And admitting too, that, despite my misgivings, I'm one of those hundreds of thousands for whom the heady cocktail of sociability, snow and sliding is an addictive draw each winter. For all that my favourite skiing is in the back-country, ideally alone or hanging back from the pack, by far the majority is on the groomed pistes that are the manufactured playgrounds of middle-class folk like me.

Perhaps it was the Arcadian nature of our situation that explains why the news hit me so hard. I suspect the subliminal unease in our privilege plays a part too. Of course, it might simply have been the shock of the unthinkable... But whatever the reason, when my son said *'have you seen that they've full-on invaded Ukraine'* it suddenly all felt so wrong.

In the passing of that one sentence, the contrast between the beauty of our location and the horror of wider circumstance became all too clear. The thought of finishing our food only to career carefree down the slopes seemed grossly inappropriate. I wanted to get back, to return home and take comfort in those I loved...

But, if I'm honest, my heart sank for less noble reasons too.

The prospect of another crisis—on top of Brexit and the pandemic and the rising cost of living—surfaced deep, if selfish, anxieties. Will we ever, I wondered, be free of this grinding uncertainty? Is our yearning for security, like Helen Keller claimed, 'mostly superstition'—out of reach of the children of men? Her assertion may well be right in fact, but the longing is real and heartfelt, for few of us are truly stoic by nature.

These last two weeks I've limited my exposure to popular news and certainly avoided social media. Not because I want to hide away but because I'm wary of their amplification of the noise and its impact on my own, and indeed our collective, wellbeing. I know too well the process of generating stories and constructing narratives that do little to improve our knowledge but a lot to worsen our worries.

Quiet reflection, coupled with a steely resolve to stand by our conclusions, is not what sells newspapers, generates clicks or raises viewer ratings. And yet—for me at least—this internal reasoning is what's most needed to find peace with, rather than panic in, the actions we must now take.

The historian Yuval Noah Harari spends weeks each year on meditative retreats to see things as they really are. That's not an appropriate response to an international crisis, but perhaps there's something in it for our coming to terms with the long-term implications of the course we must follow. Might it also help put into perspective our other worries and fixations? As I write these words, I'm conscious that Brexit, the pandemic, the cost of living... all seem so trivial compared to what's happening a mere few hundred miles from Berlin.

Perhaps then, a tangential benefit of this upheaval is that we might find the courage to focus more on what really matters—not just in geo-politics but in our daily lives too. Is it just possible that in facing into issues that are existentially vital we might begin to abandon our obsessions with the inconsequential and worry less about what cannot be changed? Some of us might even learn to give more thanks for the overwhelming (and largely unearned) good fortune we enjoy?

It has taken me a fortnight to be able to write this post, the issues—and the feelings they evoke—shapeshifting in my mind. Only gradually has my heartbeat slowed. But with its calming has come a greater acceptance of the realities of the world and the potential for evil which deep down we always knew was there. There's an affirmation too of what needs to be done and a resolve to see it through rather than wish it away. In some strange way, it almost feels good to have this clarity forced upon us.

So no denial for sure.

Though curiously, and certainly unexpectedly, in reflecting these last two weeks, I've found myself more hopeful than I might have imagined. If the situation in Ukraine gets worse by the day there is, I sense, a flicker (if not quite a flame) of optimism in the exposure of our delusions and the galvanising shock of a truth that's been hiding in plain sight. There's a refreshing honesty too in the equally plain actions we've taken, and a rare pride in the unity of democratic governments and their recommitment to principles we'd let slide for too long. Am I alone in feeling that this wake-up call is a chance to reset our values (and our policies) to ones that are ethically sound rather than economically convenient?

This week I'm in Majorca, on a cycle camp that was first booked pre-pandemic. The very fact I'm here on holiday feels more poignant and privileged than it would have three weeks previously. Yesterday, as we rode in the warmth of a soft spring sun one of our group spoke unprompted of the delight she took in her retirement, listing her blessings—financial and otherwise—for all who cared to listen.

I didn't reply, but I counted my own, more aware than ever of the myriad protections that insulate me and my family from the cold realities faced by millions elsewhere. And as I did so—and this, I promise, is no word of a lie—I looked up from the wheel I'd been following, only to realise that we were riding through a field of poppies.

The traces we leave

Earlier this week I disposed of an old bedside cabinet at our house in France. It was one of those items you feel guilty for dumping, but deep down know the charity shop won't want either. For the last two years, it's stood by our front door so the postman can leave small parcels. When the mice took up residence, it was time to let go.

But as is the way here, recycling it meant removing the marble top, separating the lining from its outer casing, checking each section for nails... And in so doing, discovering a photograph that, decades earlier, someone had taped to the underside of a drawer. An image of two girls looking into a lens saw its first light of day for lord knows how long.

Who'd put it there I wondered? The faces suggest they are sisters, but whose daughters or granddaughters might they be? And why paste their picture where it wouldn't be seen? Are they still with us... or gone now, like the cabinet that housed the fragment of their past?

I guess we could weave all manner of stories from such flimsy threads. But that's what novelists do, and I'm not one of those.

So instead I pondered the traces we leave...

My neighbour is a mason who restores historic buildings—every time I see him at work I'm in awe. Like many craftsmen, he brushes off praise. But if you asked, he'd explain the tradition of mason's marks and how to find 'signatures' in the stone of cathedral walls. His imprint will endure for generations.

Many years ago my mother wrote a song for her primary school class. One of my earliest memories is her figuring the tune on chime bars at our home. It's since been published in dozens of hymn books and is widely recorded around the world. By the time she dies, how many hundreds of thousands will have sung 'I listen and I listen'? No doubt, we will play it at her funeral.

And what will I leave?

Some writing perhaps, at least for as long as it lasts; there are two obscure rock climbs I've given a name to; perhaps someone will keep one of my paintings... Jane and I like to think that every house we've owned has benefited from our stewardship. With luck, there'll be some inheritance...

But beyond these tangibilities?

Very little I hope. For legacies are not the purpose of life or indeed the best measure of our contributions. There's value in making a difference now: in helping and healing, in supporting and providing; in simply making ends meet so that those we love can flourish. In an age when we're so driven to 'succeed', some say we should live more in the moment.

Though by historical standards, we generally do. I read somewhere that very few of us know the forenames of our great grandparents; after three generations we're lost to memory. That seems to me no bad thing, for I've always thought the veneration of ancestors to be misplaced. If I could visit any time in history, I'd choose the future, not the past.

As I write the conclusion to this post, I'm struck that my doing so has been delayed.

Why?

Because for a week I lost the picture of the girls, absentmindedly putting it down to watch the contrails in the sky across our valley. Had I not tidied up, it would have curled and faded in the sunlight that streams through the window. Every day here, the planes go back and forth... a web of slipstreams that momentarily sparkle, then fade to oblivion.

Hope

Why would anyone climb a mountain?

'Because it's there', was George Malory's famous riposte when asked about attempting Everest. And to some extent he's right. But for all its pith, his answer does little to explain the subtler motivations of those of us who set our sights on lesser peaks.

I was reminded of this at the weekend when I went to North Wales with my rock climbing club. We camped under Tryfan in the Ogwen Valley, one of the most beautiful yet starkest in Snowdonia. There were ten of us in all: four novices, some accomplished leaders and me, who I guess you might class as a late returner—historically experienced, but distinctly lacking in practice!

In truth, I was lacking in more than that. Strength, for one thing, diminishes with age, as does flexibility and perhaps most importantly confidence, which is impervious to bluff. Hence I was glad that my eldest son had come along to be my partner. We've climbed together a few times this summer, the roles gradually shifting from me as mentor to him as front runner on the rope.

On Saturday we headed to Cwm Idwal, where its eponymous slabs host some of the valley's best known routes. The 'Ordinary' may be the easiest on the crag, but it's still five pitches of balance and counterpoise, requiring trust and technique to tackle it safely. Daniel was aware I'd once climbed it with his mum. What he didn't know is that the lake below the cliff is where we'd walked hand in hand in the January rain and knew—with a certainty borne of love—that there was no going back.

Two years later we were married in a chapel at Betws y Coed, coming to the lake the day after our wedding as a sort of pilgrimage to its power. Another time, we found a red rose lodged in a crack on the slabs, and with it a note from a girl to her boyfriend who'd died in the Himalayas.

All this came back as I climbed—slowly and without much elegance—on Saturday.

But there is more to our passion than speed or style. Indeed this weekend one party had a late finish, requiring a descent in the dark that will no doubt live in their memory. And happily so, for all were safe and smiling on their return, bonded not broken by the experience. Just as all the best climbing should be.

Another member scrambled up Tryfan only to drive thirty miles south to Cadair Idris and jog to its summit. That's over 5,000 feet in a day: dismay for some; a delight for those who are able. How I wish that ever I were... Mountains are about more than ropes and harnesses.

This weekend I saw walkers and cyclists, runners and kayakers, cake eating tourists (me among them) and families exploring the lower paths. There was even a hot air balloon inflated at night at Capel Curig! On the way to Idwal we passed a woman with twisted hips, each step a labour of effort, leaning on her sticks every few yards. As we went by she beamed the broadest of smiles.

And then, there are the new friendships I made, the views at dusk, the marvelling at the Milky Way... the sheer bloody joy of being in such a special place. It's been said we climb mountains, not for the views from the top, but from the bottom. Those who love the hills, or know any landscape intimately, will understand what that's getting at.

On Sunday I was tired, my son's girlfriend joined us and wanted to climb too. I was glad, for I felt in some intangible way that my part was done; that it was their turn now. They headed back to Cwm Idwal to climb a different but parallel line to the one I'd chosen the day before. It would be their memory, not mine, their time and their experience together.

The route was called Hope.

CHANT:
AN AFTERWORD

Of all the advice I offer to would be bloggers, and of all the ambitions I have for my writing, the subject of this end piece is the most important and yet the hardest to pin down. Perhaps that's why I've been putting it off. I've said before that I write mainly from notions, trusting in direction but never sure of destination. As I sit at my desk this morning I sense the rare discomfort of the opposite—of being clear in my terminus, but as good as lost in how to get there.

But then, it's not about me!

And that in a nutshell is the conclusion on which I'm so clear and yet am struggling to show my workings for. The bareness of my margins reminds of those savants who multiply complex numbers but are unable to explain how they do it—and of my friend whose kayaking brilliance was so intuitive that when we took to filming his technique he couldn't recognise or compute what he saw. The point I'm making is not that I'm a savant or a genius—oh, the shame that I might have hinted as much— it's that not only are my margins blank, but that should I have pens and pages galore I'd still have little to show.

For what I'm struggling with here isn't writer's block, it's finding a succinct way of describing the difference between writing *about* our experience, as opposed to writing *from* it. And though this is subtle, it's vital, and especially so in the first person medium of blogging.

The former—writing *about* ourselves and our lives—is focused on the 'me': it's all about what I saw, what I did, what I think… Writing this way may purport to look outward, but more often it's a mirror to vanity, presenting our egos in a carefully composed tableau that's as static and posed as a Victorian photograph.

But the latter—writing *from* our experience—inverts this perspective, drawing on events and emotions which may at times be deeply personal, but with the hope of sparking a connection whose energy is charged by the reader as much as the author. It's this circuitry that makes both writing and reading worthwhile—that gives it electricity if you like—and in the case blogging, elevates it above the mere transmission of opinion and reportage.

It's not about me.

Just as Orwell's essays are not really about him; he died long ago and yet his words are (mostly) as relevant and fresh today as they were in the Thirties. The same is true of Montaigne, or Ruskin, or Hazlitt or any of the great historical essayists. The connections they spark are as alive today as ever—so much so that in reading the best of them we get the sense that their insights are what we've been thinking all along. Which is why…

It's not about me.

My good friend, the writer and lecturer Tim Gibson, said to me recently that our entitlement to expressing opinions is something we are best minded to earn rather than assert. He wasn't claiming this in a political or philosophic sense; rather he was referring to the decades he'd spent writing columns for motor magazines, and to the training and academic study that underpinned his ordination as a priest. Without those foundations, what claim did he have to be an expert in his fields—and why would anyone want to listen to him? It was a typically thoughtful way of expressing what one of my early tutors had put more bluntly—'Unless you're famous, nobody cares about you.'

It's not about me.

As writers, we are urged to show not tell: *don't say it's stormy, describe the turning up of your collar, the bending into the wind.* The idea is that the reader fills the gaps with a richness of imagery that's more real and resonant than any closed description. As bloggers this advice should extend beyond mere narration, into the questions we pose, the emotions we share, the paths we follow—and those we might have chosen.

Because what readers really care about is not our truth or our opinion, or even our experience—it's whether the words they are reading resonate with their lives and concerns. As writers, we can choose to show ourselves and our vulnerabilities—and indeed to do so is often powerful—but it is narcissism or hubris or both to think that's enough.

Sufficiency lies not merely in displaying what we've found but in helping others make their own discoveries. This is what elevates our blogs—and our writing more generally—from the personal to the universal.

It's not about me.

That's the mantra I recite as surely as mediative devotees chant Om.

And like all contemplation, it takes time to sink in. For as with any practice of this sort—from prayer to painting, or even to brooding—there's an experiential element that transcends pat formulas. In writing *from* our experience, we must listen to the tone of our words, pay attention to their flow, and like a potter at a wheel, 'feel' our way to a greater awareness if not exactly enlightenment.

Which is why I'm not going to fill my margins after all—because I've realised that this book is full of them; that *Views from the Bike Shed* is my workings out laid bare. The successes and failures are there for all to see: in its messy and misjudged experiments: in the reflective questions, the turns in perspective; the uses of 'could' in place of 'ought'… From my quirky punctuation, to the lines I've chosen to draw—and those I've chosen not to; in my strivings and frustrations and will and care to try and try again…

It's not about me.

I say it every time I write.

Like grace before a meal.

It's not about me.

It's not about me.

It's…

Time to press 'publish'.

Acknowledgements

Writing a blog for over decade involves so many people that I'm tempted—so as not to risk omissions—to merely say thanks to all who've helped along the way. I'm mindful too that blogs are interactive and it's the readers of *Views from the Bike Shed* who have inspired and shaped my practice as much as anyone. My thanks to them.

But there are some who deserve special mention.

Michelle Chapman, my first blogging friend and now gardening writer has been a regular advisor and wise counsel. So too, in the early days, Cara Boden, whose blog about adapting to life in the Peak District showed me that great writing need not stray far from home. And more recently, Yamini Maclean who was kind enough to read parts of the manuscript and offer constructive feedback.

In the wider writing community, I owe particular thanks to Sally Baker, former director at Ty Newydd, the National Writing Centre for Wales; to Jim Perrin, our finest outdoor author, whose essays first inspired me to pick up a pen; and to Rory Maclean, for encouragement and praise that gave me more confidence than he would know.

Serendipity plays a part in all writing as well as careers—and isn't it wonderful! For how blessed was I, in the course of my working life, to commission a copywriter who turned out also to be a professor of theology, an author, a lecturer in creative writing, and later an ordained priest? Tim Gibson is among the wisest, most intelligent and certainly the kindest, people I've ever known—that I don't share his faith and yet delight in our discussions is proof positive that true friendship can (and should) transcend even the deepest of beliefs.

Which brings me to those, without whom *Views from the Bike Shed* (as both blog and book) would not have been possible.

Jan Fortune at Cinnamon Press is a force of nature and for good; her support has changed my writing life and that of many others. Serendipity and a blessing once again.

And finally my family, who've tolerated with good grace, the reinterpretation of their lives that comes with blogging about my own. To Daniel, Michael and Dylan, I offer in return the love that only Jane can match. She of course, is the silent partner in all of this; the ever present force—most often in the space between the lines—holding me and *Views from the Bike Shed* together. Ironically, words are not sufficient.

In gratitude.
Mark Charlton

Author Biography

Mark Charlton is that rare thing; a corporate professional (with a background in media distribution and marketing) and a creative writer, painter, tutor… some would say polymath.

After nearly forty years in industry, Mark retired in 2018, lasting all of ten days before starting a communications consultancy. He now divides his time between working with clients, occasional teaching and following his passions for writing, the outdoors and walking his whippet Oscar.

Mark's first book *Counting Steps—a journey through fatherhood and landscape* (Cinnamon Press 2012) was a critically acclaimed collection, exploring the transformative impact of parenthood and its connections to place and the past. His reflective honesty is allied to a concern to make life writing universal. 'I try always to write from my life as opposed to about it—for ultimately, it's not me that matters.'

Talking of his practice, Mark says, 'It took me years to be confident in what I do, rather than feeling self-conscious about what I don't. I'm not a novelist, poet or journalist; I'm a life writer, essayist and most of all, a proud and passionate blogger!'

Ingram Content Group UK Ltd.
Milton Keynes UK
UKHW012015200323
418877UK00003B/18